The Cider Book

THE

CIDER BOOK

Lila Gault and Betsy Sestrap

Madrona Publishers
Seattle

Library of Congress Cataloging in Publication Data

Gault, Lila, 1946 -
  The cider book.

  Includes index.
  1. Cider. 2. Cookery (Cider)
I. Sestrap, Betsy, 1922-   joint author
II. Title.
TX415.G38   641.2   80-18267
ISBN 0-914842-48-X

USA

Madrona Publishers, Inc.
2116 Western Avenue
Seattle, Washington 98121

CANADA

Douglas & McIntyre Ltd.
1615 Venables Street
Vancouver, B.C. V5L 2H1

For Erin and Peter,
who drink cider like most kids drink milk.

PREFACE

This project began as a collaboration between a writer/cook and a cidermaker/cook to share ideas and experiences with cider in the kitchen. Lila Gault, the writer, has for many years made apple cider and apple champagne at home. Betsy Sestrap, the cidermaker, is a partner in Wax Orchards, a commercial producer of fresh cider.

As we became more curious about the culinary potential of cider, both bottled and fresh, we found ourselves trying it in almost everything that we cooked for several months. In the process of our experiments, we developed a wide spectrum of delicious, easy-to-prepare recipes.

Although much of the book was created in our own kitchens, we learned about the traditional use of cider in cooking by investigating the cuisines of the West Country in England, Normandy and Brittany in France, and the Asturias province in Spain. Those are the regions of Europe where apples have flourished for centuries. Cider has become an integral part of those provincial cuisines in the same way that wine has been married to food wherever local vineyards can be found.

In learning to use cider in the kitchen, we learned about cider as a beverage as well. We watched the production of fresh cider at Wax Orchards and journeyed abroad to see the production of bottled cider firsthand. We also learned to control the natural fermentation of fresh cider at home for use in cooking and as a beverage. Finally we tasted and evaluated bottled ciders to use in the kitchen and to drink by the glass.

We hope this book not only will eliminate some of the prevalent confusion about cider, but also will allow cider of all types to earn its rightful place in the kitchens and on the tables of today's cooks.

September 1980
Lila Gault
Betsy Sestrap

ACKNOWLEDGMENTS

We are enormously grateful to our friends whose contributions and support enabled a good idea to become a good book. Special thanks go to Ron Irvine at Pike and Western Wines in Seattle, Tom Stockley, wine columnist at the Seattle *Times*, Robert L. LaBelle, Professor of Food Science at Cornell University, Fred Arterberry Jr. at the Arterberry Ciderworks in McMinnville, Oregon, and Susan Wallace on Bainbridge Island.

Robert Sestrap contributed valuable technical advice on cider making and Mac Kennedy used his culinary genius to create some of the tastiest recipes in the book. Both gentlemen also devoted many meals to the evaluation of cider recipes.

And particular thanks to our publisher, Dan Levant, for his unflagging enthusiasm and support for this project.

Contents

The Cider Book

CHAPTER 1

Cider Traditions

When most of us think about apple cider, visions of crisp fall days, trees burdened with red sun-ripened fruit, and roadside stands stacked with jugs of golden liquid come to mind. This is the cider of autumn, the drink that is traditionally served to the hordes of thirsty children who knock expectantly on neighborhood doors in search of an annual Halloween treat. For skiers and football fans, it's hot cider with a shot of rum, to take the chill off a windy afternoon. And in recent years, cider has become the beverage of choice for those who favor wholesome natural food and drink.

In fact, we are probably more likely to agree on our feelings about cider than on the nature of the drink itself. Even the basic definition of fresh cider causes some disagreement. The one that we prefer is perhaps the most simple.

Fresh sweet cider is the natural liquid that is released or expressed by pressing finely chopped or ground fruit. Although apples are the most common fruit from which cider is made, pears and sweet cherries are often pressed for cider as well. That liquid is fresh cider as long as it remains in its natural state and is not sweetened, preserved, clarified or otherwise altered. As the natural fermentation process runs its course, the cider remains cider at every step of the way.

Fresh sweet cider is converted into what is commonly labelled and sold as apple juice by pasteurizing and the addition of preservatives that stop the fermentation process for a month or longer. Apple juice can also be made by pasteurizing clarified cider at 195 degrees Fahrenheit for one minute. These procedures produce a liquid with relatively long shelf life and no other significant advantages. Apple juice is a cider derivative with very little resemblance to its source in intensity or general quality of flavor. Even though some producers label apple juice as cider, especially during the fall, apple juice is simply not cider.

Fresh apple cider is always (sometimes very) sweet in taste, amber to golden in color, opaque in appearance, aromatic in odor and entirely non-alcoholic. However, this description only strictly applies to the first hours (or days when refrigerated) of the beverage's life. Fresh apple cider is a lively and occasionally volatile liquid that can change many aspects of its distinctive character practically overnight.

As fresh cider is separated from the ground pulp of the apple with a machine-powered or hand-operated press, wild yeasts that are naturally present on the skin of the fruit are swept along into the liquid. These yeasts begin to change the natural sugar in the liquid into alcohol. The natural fermentation process is most often described as *turning, working* or *hardening.*

Cider ferments very rapidly and sometimes even violently at temperatures above 50 degrees Fahrenheit. The process is more leisurely and the results much smoother when the temperature around the working cider is 40 degrees or less. As fermentation converts the sugar into alcohol and the solid particles slowly settle, the sweetness begins to subside and the cider appears clearer and lighter in color.

The beverage that results from the natural fermentation process is the cider of pioneer North America, produced in great quantities wherever farmers had apples. Our forefathers were proud of their cider production and they eagerly anticipated a good annual supply. The mildly alcoholic beverage was not only a pleasure to drink, but also a most convenient and easy means of preserving the usually bountiful apple harvest.

Even those who relish the clean refreshing taste of fresh cider often misunderstand the complexities of the beverage in its different stages of natural fermentation. The prevailing confusion, found today from coast to coast in much of the United States, is partly the result of political turmoil, as well as a decided shift in national flavor preferences.

Naturally fermented "hard" cider was a staple of life in the United States from the earliest colonial times until the mid-nineteenth-century temperance campaigns that resulted in the destruction of thousands of acres of apple orchards. By the turn of the century, hard cider had all but disappeared from the national diet. The return, now, of fresh sweet cider to the nation's tables and kitchens has brought wide acceptance for the beverage in its sweet state, but many of the most enthusiastic cider lovers mistakenly consider the beverage spoiled as soon as fermentation begins. As a result, unfortunately, tasty, good cider is often thrown away.

The cider of the pioneers was not unlike what is now produced for the commercial market in Canada and Australia, as well as in England, France and other countries in western Europe. Bottled cider is a clear and usually straw-colored liquid which is effervescent in character and often somewhat fruity in taste. Bottled ciders are, in fact, apple wines with a wide variety of alcohol content. The heady cider known as scrumpy, sold from barrels in pubs throughout Devon and Somerset in England, runs as high as 10 percent, but most bottled ciders are a more modest 3 to 6 percent alcohol.

American winemakers are beginning to show great interest in bottled cider, and those with easy access to good cider apples are making cider with great success. The size of their production keeps the market strictly local, but the popularity of bottled cider has encouraged these winemakers to keep the cider coming.

The sweetness of different bottled ciders varies almost as greatly as the alcohol content. Since most bottled cider has sugar added during the fermentation process to establish sufficient alcohol content to prevent spoilage, there will occasionally be some residual sugar in the finished product. More frequently though, the cider has its sweetener added in the blending process just before bottling. Some ciders are left in a dry, more natural state.

European ciders are made from particularly tart and coarse apples grown especially for cider making. These apples give a distinctively sharp and sometimes bitter taste to the cider that results. Bottled cider made in Canada and the United States begins with juice pressed from the culls of table apples. In Australia, one large cidermaker blends a concentrate pressed from English apples with locally grown apples for a milder yet definitely Old World taste.

World production of bottled cider exceeds 140 million gallons (U.S. measure) a year. Cider is the table drink of the apple-growing regions throughout western Europe. The popularity of cider there is historic and involves considerable tradition and lore. Barrels of cider sit next to barrels of stout, ale and beer in pubs throughout Devon, Somerset and Cornwall in England. A carafe of cider is often served on dinner tables in Normandy and Brittany, as wine is found elsewhere in France. Asturias on the coast of northern Spain counts cider as its significant contribution to Spanish cuisine.

While some Europeans and Canadians might sit down to meals with bottled cider, Americans are more likely to serve fresh sweet cider directly from the press. Let's take a look at the production of fresh cider at a large cider mill in the Pacific Northwest, and then journey to France and on to Australia for a look at cider abroad.

CIDER MAKING IN NORTH AMERICA

It is a fifteen-minute drive from the Vashon Island ferry dock to the 250-acre farm called Wax Orchards. Seattle is just a short ferry ride away, but the island's remaining forests and well-fenced pastures have an air of timeless tranquility that belies their urban proximity. It is a perfect setting for the largest fresh cider mill in the Pacific Northwest.

Cider is only the most recent product of Wax Orchards, an enterprise that began in 1929 when August and Johanna Wax came to the island from a farming community just south of Seattle with a mind to raise pie cherries. They bought a large tract of land that had been logged once, cleared away the second-growth timber and logging debris, and planted Montmorency cherry trees. They enjoyed decades of successful cherry harvests and planted several acres of peach trees as well. The next logical addition to the orchardists' acreage was apples. Another thirty acres went into apple trees of many different varieties.

The Waxes discovered that unlike cherries and peaches, which brought a good return, their apples found little or no market as table fruit. Rainy western Washington simply would not produce the picture-book fruit grown just across the Cascade Mountains in the irrigated orchards of the Yakima Valley. They could barely meet expenses with their Gravenstein, Golden Delicious, and Stayman apples, which were juicy and delicious, but small and irregular by eastern Washington standards.

Cider seemed to be an obvious use for the unsold apples and a large old wine press was put into use. Neighbors and friends were the first customers, but as the word spread, demand for the cider far outstripped the supply.

Then in 1970, the family got an unexpected prod from nature when a severe hailstorm damaged most of that season's apples. Faced with a bruised apple crop that could only be saved by making cider, and a press which produced only a few gallons at a time, the cidermakers decided to mechanize the process. A simple fifteen-ton press and a mill for grinding the apples were built to increase production capability. Almost 8,000 U.S. gallons of cider were pressed and sold that year. Not a single good apple grown at Wax Orchards has escaped the cider jug since.

Visitors to Wax Orchards park their cars next to the comfortable two-story farmhouse and walk a few hundred feet out to the cannery building where, on almost any day of the week, cider making is in progress.

Five or six people are hard at work in an 11,000-square-foot cement block building which was constructed as a cannery for the cherries and peaches. The workers are warmly dressed in order to remain comfortable in the unheated structure.

The roar of the machinery makes conversation almost impossible even at the opposite end of the cannery. A strong fruity smell of apples pervades the air. Visitors are advised to wear boots because on pressing days the concrete floor of the cannery is usually wet. Both the cold and dampness can be escaped inside a small office, where a woodstove is usually burning and a pot of hot cider sits ready to be poured.

Several dozen big bins of apples sit near a large loading dock, some inside the building and others on the ground. Each bin holds half a ton of fruit. In the fall, the bins are full of apples harvested from the farm's orchards by neighbor kids and migrant pickers. Many of these red, green and yellow apples have simply fallen, as apples will when they are fully ripened and ready for the cider press. Others have been picked up from the ground after the tree has been lightly shaken.

The full bins are hauled from the orchard on a trailer which has been especially designed to run behind a large farm tractor. The tractor can move ten bins at once and can bring much of the daily harvest to the cannery in two or three trips.

A single bin is positioned on a hydraulic lift which tilts gradually until the apples begin to spill out onto a scrubber and then into a hopper filled with water. A worker is on hand to keep an even stream of apples flowing into the bath and to see that all the apples are thoroughly washed.

The apples are pushed toward a paddle wheel by several jets of water at the far end of the bath. The paddle wheel guides the apples onto a conveyor which moves them slowly past more jets and up to another worker. The apples are carefully inspected for spoilage, and any bad parts are removed or the whole fruit discarded if necessary. This stream of apples flows steadily under the worker's watchful eye into a mill where it is ground to the consistency of applesauce. Fine grinding reduces oxidation and also allows the maximum amount of cider to be released from the pulp when it is pressed.

The pomace, as the ground apples are called, plops into fifty-five-gallon steel drums with plastic liners. Each barrel is labelled by the variety of apple that it holds. Some of the pomace heads directly for the press and the rest is stored in a freezer for use during the weeks and months ahead. By freezing freshly ground apple pulp for later use, Wax Orchards is able to make fresh cider throughout the year.

The juice of three to six different varieties of apples is carefully blended for Wax Orchards cider. Sweet and tart apples are always combined to create a balanced and full-bodied product. The formula demands 40 to 50 percent juice from tart apples. A consistent balance is maintained throughout the year by using pomace stored in the freezer. Most cider mills do not have this capability and must make cider strictly from available apples, whose sweetness can vary substantially according to the variety and the time of year.

When enough barrels have been filled with different varieties of apple pulp, the press is put into action. The press operator stacks several oak racks and forms in a large stainless steel tray designed to hold the cider as it is pressed from the pulp. Each form is lined with a coarsely woven nylon cloth, which is laid in place carefully to keep it smooth and straight. Several buckets of pomace are poured onto the cloth, then the corners are folded and the form is removed. A rack is placed on top of the so-called cheese, another form is put in place, and the process is repeated.

When the press operator is finished there will be ten to twelve cheeses in the stack. The weight of the cheeses on top causes liquid to run freely from those on the bottom of the pile and the metal tray fills quickly with cider before the press is even started. The presser pushes the loaded stack under the press, flips a switch and 30,000 pounds of pressure are gradually applied to the apple pulp by a hydraulic system.

As the cider cascades from the pomace, a pump is started which carries the liquid through a clear plastic tube to the cooling tanks, which are located on a platform above the bottling area. As many as ninety gallons of cider will be collected from a single pressing.

The cider passes through a fine screen mesh to strain any stray pieces of pulp from the liquid and then flows into a holding tank where it is quickly chilled and stored at 33 degrees Fahrenheit. It passes through a second screen en route to a dairy-style filling machine which fills and caps quart, half-gallon and gallon plastic bottles. The jugs are stored at just above freezing until the next day when they are delivered by refrigerated truck to nearly two hundred retail and restaurant accounts in the Puget Sound area.

Variations of the activity at Wax Orchards can be found in communities across the United States. Some East Coast cider mills have been in business for several generations. Others, like Wax Orchards, have opened their doors more recently in response to the public demand for fresh cider.

All successful cider making follows several general rules, whether the press is a neighborhood gathering place or the center of a large commercial operation. When the basic rules are followed, good results are assured.

Only whole, firm and properly ripened apples should be used in the production of cider. An apple that is ready to fall from the tree will be at its peak of juiciness and natural sugar. Windfalls should be examined carefully, however. Apples that are soiled or rotten will make cider that is foul and rough.

Good cider is blended from several different types of apples. Certain varieties of apples have special characteristics that work together to make a fully balanced and flavorful cider. Jonathan and Winesap apples, for example, are rather tart, and Gravensteins are very juicy. Others, such as Red Delicious, 20 Ounce, and Stayman, add body to the blend.

Sugar, acidity and juiciness are the important characteristics of good cider apples. Although backyard cidermakers usually press only those apples that are readily available, commercial producers often blend the earlier apples of summer, which are usually tart, with the later, sweeter varieties to blend a balanced cider.

The use of sound ripe apples of different varieties, and most important, cleanliness at every step during the process, insures good fresh cider. The fruit must be washed very thoroughly to remove the dust and residue deposited on the apples during the summer. Whether the equipment is a small hand cranked chipper and press or a large and efficient electrically powered machine, it must be scrubbed and rinsed carefully before and after it is used. A gallon of fresh sweet cider requires not only eleven to fourteen pounds of apples but several gallons of wash water as well.

Fresh cider will remain in its sweet full-bodied state for ten days to several weeks if it is stored at 38 degrees or less, which is the average temperature of a properly functioning kitchen refrigerator. The cool temperature postpones but does not prevent the natural fermentation process. Once this process begins, cider becomes a number of different beverages, tasty by the glass and amazingly useful in the kitchen.

Each jug of cider will move at its own individual rate into a semi-dry state according to its balance of sugar, acid and yeast. Yeasts that give the best flavor to fermenting cider are encouraged to grow at temperatures of 40 degrees or less. Those that give the rough and strong taste often associated with fermenting cider are discouraged by cool temperatures. While the 40-degree guideline for proper storage does not guarantee successful fermentation every time, clean cider that is carefully made and treated well will rarely just "go bad."

Lower storage temperature not only favors the better flavored yeasts, but also slows the rate at which the natural sugar is turned into alcohol. A slower fermentation process results in smoother and more flavorful semi-dry and dry hard cider.

Fresh cider should be exposed to air as little as possible. Contact with oxygen eventually turns fermenting cider into acetic acid or vinegar, although this may not happen for three or four months. A container of fermenting cider should have its cap slightly loosened to permit carbon dioxide to escape, but care should be taken that the caps are barely rather than very loose.

The first stage of natural fermentation, *semi-dry*, seems to be the favorite among those who appreciate fresh cider as a beverage. The cider is usually quite effervescent as a result of the fermentation process, and noticeably drier than when it was first pressed. Alcohol content is slight, usually no more than 3 percent, but the flavor and fruitiness of the cider is usually substantial.

The second, or *dry hard*, stage of fermentation often takes weeks of storage in cool temperatures. Dry hard cider is bone dry and 6 or 7 percent alcohol, since all of the natural sugar has been changed by the yeasts into alcohol. Dry hard cider is naturally quite clear and if stored for weeks after the fermentation is complete, it will become completely clear as the minute particles of apple pulp sink to the bottom of the jug. Some fruitiness may be evident in certain ciders at this stage, but most have virtually no apple flavor. Effervescence also disappears when full fermentation is finally reached.

Naturally fermented dry hard cider, which was served daily on country tables from colonial times until the early years of this century in the United States, is almost unknown as a table beverage today. Since naturally fully fermented cider is not a commercial product, only those who press or buy fresh cider and then commit the time and storage space for proper fermentation will be able to enjoy it at all. Those cidermakers are rewarded, however, with more than just a refreshing drink. Naturally fermented cider is exempt from the federal tax regulations which apply to large quantities of homemade wine and beer.

But even a profitable tax break isn't really enough incentive to inspire potential retailers of naturally fermented hard cider. First of all, space-consuming refrigeration is required to prevent the cider from spoiling or fermenting too quickly. Even with proper refrigeration, the relatively low alcohol content of the beverage makes it difficult to keep for more than a short period of time.

Although it is impractical for most of us to make naturally fermented cider in great quantity, it is both effortless and most rewarding to buy a gallon or two of fresh cider, leave it in the kitchen refrigerator to ferment for a few weeks, and then put it to use, as we would wine, in the kitchen.

CIDER MAKING ABROAD

The production and enjoyment of cider is a centuries-old tradition throughout the apple-growing regions of France, England, Spain and other countries of western Europe. It is a tradition steeped in folklore and custom, and it has spawned nearly as many stories and legends as enthusiasts for one of the world's oldest beverages.

In England it is said that Joseph of Arimathea came to Glastonbury in Somerset to found a center of Christianity in the years following the death of Christ. Glastonbury was known in Arthurian times as Avalon, which means the isle of apples. Joseph was said to have eaten apples at Glastonbury and then spat the seeds into Somerset. Cider-apple trees sprang from the ground as a result and created the vast orchards that grow today in Hereford, Somerset and Devon.

English villagers in Somerset still practice the traditional ritual of apple wassailing, which is supposed to ensure a bountiful crop. On January 6, Twelfth Night, they gather around the largest tree in the orchard, drink to its health, and pour cider over its roots. Then everyone joins hands and dances around the tree while some blast shotguns in the air to scare evil spirits away. Pieces of cider-soaked bread are tied to the tree's branches as an offering to robins, the good spirits of the tree.

There are nearly 300 different varieties of cider apples growing in England today, some of which are descendants of ancient trees first planted by the Romans. Most have picturesque names like Slack-My-Girdle, Lady's Finger, Cats' Heads, and Sheep's Nose. Their juice produces the bittersweet flavor characteristic of English cider. These apples are sour, bitter and coarse by the standards for most table or eating apples, but they are the absolutely essential raw material for proper English cider.

The juice from those apples is so essential to cider that H.P. Bulmer Ltd., the largest producer by volume of cider in the world, exports it in concentrated form to its plants in other countries, including a large operation located in Campbelltown, New South Wales, Australia, which was opened in 1969.

The concentrate is shipped halfway around the world and reconstituted and blended with fresh juice from apples grown in Tasmania and other parts of Australia. A typical batch of cider from Bulmer/Australia is 40 percent from apple concentrate pressed at the orchards near the main plant in Hereford, England. The blended juice is inoculated with a special wine yeast which has been isolated and kept pure for almost a hundred years.

Then the cider ferments for several weeks in huge 10,000 and 20,000 gallon tanks which, following Herefordshire tradition at the original cider works, are named for towns or people involved in the long history of the firm. The large tanks are called Sydney, Adelaide, Brisbane, Koala, Kanza and Credenhill and the smaller ones are labelled Patrick, James Cook and David, for example.

Each tank ferments at a slightly different rate which is controlled by the surrounding temperature as the tanks are not refrigerated. Once fermentation is completed, the cider is allowed to settle and siphoned off to rest. After some days it goes into a centrifuge for clarification and then is passed through a diatomaceous-earth filter and finally through a filter of special paper. Then the cider is ready for blending.

The cider is blended with water to create an alcohol content that depends on the label under which it will be sold. Carbonation also varies according to the label and is done as the cider is bottled. The bottles are filled at the rate of eight hundred gallons an hour and are pasteurized briefly before they are labelled and put into cases for shipping.

The original Bulmer cider works in Hereford began operation in 1888. Four thousand gallons of cider were made that year in a rented warehouse by Percy Bulmer, an enterprising twenty-year-old. His brother soon joined the successful business and by 1911, the Bulmers were granted a Royal Warrant, making them the official cidermakers for the British royal family.

Cider making in Hereford usually begins by mid-September and goes full tilt through October and November. The cider works uses apples from its thousands of acres of orchards, and buys still more from independent local growers. The apples are shaken from the trees and delivered to the cider mill where they are washed several times, ground to a fine pulp and pressed. The juice is stored in settling vats and then pumped into other vats for fermentation, which usually takes about three or four weeks. The storage vats, named for countries, planets, and even birds, store 15 million gallons of cider at one time. The largest tank is named Strongbow and holds 1,650,000 gallons of cider.

The other major cider-producing country of Europe is France. Much of the cider made at cider mills throughout the countryside in Normandy is turned into Calvados, the fiery brandy that is traditionally consumed after rich meals as a digestive aid. Calvados is relatively unknown outside of France, especially in comparison to the brandies made from grapes, Cognac and Armagnac. It is available in America in small quantities and is eagerly sought by connoisseurs who especially value its fruity aroma and faint apple aftertaste.

Under French law, only the apple brandy made in particular areas of Normandy can be labelled and sold as Calvados. It must be slowly aged in oak casks and approved, batch by batch, by a licensed tasting panel.

Calvados is not only an excellent sipping liqueur, but very useful in the kitchen as well. A Norman version of the traditional Burgundian *coq au vin* takes on a lively fruitiness with the addition of Calvados to the preparation. Another classic use for Calvados is in a light and frothy dessert soufflé.

We had some firsthand experience with Calvados and Normandy cider several years ago, and like most American travellers to France, we came home in search of those "liquid apples" with little success. Fortunately, cider and Calvados are now more readily available and the nostalgic traveller can relive fond memories in the kitchen at home, as we have done.

We had spent two extraordinary weeks in Paris as the guests of an

American friend who had been living in the city for several years. She was eager to show us France as few tourists have an opportunity to experience it. We spent the mornings of our days at national monuments like the Louvre and Notre Dame, and then met for lunch at a different brasserie or café every day, and a second establishment for dinner, until we had covered virtually every quarter of the city.

This gastronomical tour took us far beyond the culinary boundaries of Paris and even of the country itself. Parisian immigrants from all over the world seemed to bring the best of their native cuisine to their adopted city, and the local markets responded remarkably with the necessary ingredients. In discovering Paris with our palates, we also tasted the cuisines of Morocco, Algeria, Spain, Lebanon, Syria and even Russia and China.

Our hostess suggested that we spend our last weekend in France in a small seaside village in Normandy called Honfleur. She knew a small dockside pension in this community of fishermen and sailors that would serve us the very best Norman treatment of the daily catch. And then it was only a matter of climbing a small flight of stairs to a bed overlooking the harbor.

Perhaps more than in any other single region of France, the delectable cuisine of Normandy has evolved from foods grown and gathered locally. Norman cattle are grown not only for their well-marbled, tender meat, but also for some of the most flavorful, richest cream in Europe. One result of the abundance of cream is a corresponding abundance of cream sauces in many regional specialities.

Apples, cider and Calvados are also essential in the Norman preparation of food. Cider is used freely in sauces and poaching liquids. Calvados is also used with a liberal hand in the kitchen and is served routinely at the close of a large meal. We went to Normandy that weekend with great expectations of delicious cuisine and were treated to cider, Calvados, fresh cream and fresh fish in a manner and quantity that far exceeded our hopes.

Several hundred fishing boats were moored securely in Honfleur's harbor on the afternoon we arrived. Their day's work was completed, if in fact they had ventured out at all. Fishermen often sat out the cold, rainy January days in local cafés. We parked our car on the main street which ran along the harbor and got out to explore on foot. There was laughter drifting into the street from the closest cafe and we decided to investigate.

The bar was lined with friendly faces who spoke as little English as we did French. It didn't seem to matter much to anyone though, as we ordered two of the small glasses filled with Calvados that almost everyone else was drinking. While most of the patrons sipped slowly on their drinks, one brave soul opened his mouth as wide as he could, tilted his head back and tossed the entire contents of the glass into his throat with one graceful motion. As he swallowed and drew a deep breath, a cheer went up from his companions and the woman behind the bar leaned over to fill his glass again.

We finished our drinks and headed into the street in search of the pension. It was dark and our dinner reservation was for 6:30. A very small sign above the door of a narrow, four-story building identified it as our destination and a friendly large woman greeted us at the door. She spoke no English, she declared immediately in French, and understood very little. Our French got us upstairs to our room and aware of her admonition to be prompt for dinner.

Although our friend in Paris had advised us of the quantity of food we would be served at every course we were still unprepared for the largesse and culinary extravagance that was set before us. There were a dozen other diners, mostly local residents who ate regularly at this "simple" restaurant. The owner remained in the dining area through much of the meal, assisting the two young men who were serving and making sure that all of the diners were thoroughly satisfied.

Shortly after we were seated, a large pitcher of cider and two glasses were placed on the table. This was customary in restaurants throughout the region, we were told. The light, fruity cider was an excellent accompaniment to the entire meal, especially the poached sole served with a rich and flavorful cream sauce and the veal chops baked in a delicious and slightly piquant brown sauce. Both entrees were prepared, we learned later, with cider-based sauces, and Calvados was added to the sauce for the veal.

After the entrees we were offered a glass of Calvados, which is the traditional method in Normandy for dividing a long meal into two more moderate repasts. The *trou normand,* or Norman hole, is intended not only to interrupt the progress of the meal, but to create a hole in the stomach so that the diners can continue to eat even more.

We left Honfleur after two more days of glorious feasting and returned to Paris to catch a flight home. It had been a magical two weeks, given almost entirely to eating and drinking and making new discoveries. Of all the new discoveries, none was more memorable than cider.

CHAPTER 2

Buying Cider

One evening last fall, nearly a dozen of us sat around a large table, well supplied with wine glasses, scoresheets and pens, and spent several hours systematically tasting the alcoholic contents of one tall thin bottle after another. An unexpected visitor would probably have thought that we were tasting wine. But although the bottles had been purchased from local wine shops, they were filled with cider. We were tasting a variety of locally available bottled ciders, most of which had been imported from England, Canada and France.

We were all somewhat knowledgeable about wine, which gave us some preliminary understanding of the ciders. It was apparent that although bottled cider and wine share certain similar characteristics, cider has its own distinct charm.

The evening passed quickly as each taster worked intently to judge and evaluate the different ciders. Finally the scoresheets, which had been filled with cryptic notes and numbers, were handed in for tally. As we said goodnight, someone predicted that bottled cider would become as popular in America as it is in England and France.

Bottled cider, with its pleasant effervescence and mild alcoholic content, is now widely available in major cities throughout North America, as we had anticipated when that first tasting was organized last fall. Americans are greeting bottled cider with the same enthusiasm that has been shown for fresh cider during the past ten years. Cider is now a feature in many wine shops and restaurants, as well as in stores that specialize in wholesome foods.

All ciders, both bottled and fresh, not only originate from the same natural source but share certain other characteristics as well. As you learn to identify and appreciate these qualities, you will not only find great enjoyment in tasting different kinds of cider — both imported and domestic — but will develop a palate for cider that will guide you reliably in future buying.

Some of the qualities that are usually sought in good wine are also descriptive of bottled cider. For example: flavor, body, and balance between acid and sugar. Many basic elements of good wine are found in most ciders, even though cider is generally blended for uniformity and, unlike wine, does not improve with bottle age. Although the elements of character, style and substance are rarely as complex or sophisticated in cider as they are in wine, their existence gives a basis for comparison among ciders as well as a terminology familiar to wine lovers who have turned their interest to cider.

A comparative tasting of bottled ciders is both an enjoyable and instructive experience. There need be no mandatory protocol with respect to number of participants or varieties of cider. Scoring tended to be somewhat arbitrary and superfluous in our experience at several tastings last year. It is more helpful to simply make notes with certain specific characteristics in mind and then record an overall general impression. Discussion among tasters proved to be very helpful as well.

The most easily identified characteristic of bottled cider is the *balance* between sweetness and acidity. In certain parts of Canada, bottled cider is likely to be minimally sweet because much Canadian cider is produced in Ontario and Quebec, where the French influence affects cider. In the United States, however, most bottled cider — especially that imported from western Canada, England and France — is moderately to markedly sweet. The drier varieties are noticeably absent in most retail outlets in the U.S. in part because those ciders are in great demand in their countries of origin and there is little available for export; also, the marketing specialists at the large European cidermakers assume that Coca-Cola-weaned residents of the U.S. prefer sweet drinks. As a result, the cider that you may have enjoyed on a trip to France, for example, may be quite different than the cider sold under the same label at your local wine shop in the U.S.

The sweetness of bottled cider should be balanced with some acidity, and often is, especially in the more carefully made labels. The bitterness of tannin, present in the English apples grown and pressed strictly for cider, provides another aspect of balance in certain imported ciders as well.

Flavor or *fruitiness* is very desirable in bottled cider. This quality varies considerably from ciders with distinct apple character to those with absolutely no hint of any natural origin whatsoever. As an aspect of flavor, the *aftertaste* of any cider should always be smooth and pleasant. Any rough, chemical or oxidized flavor is simply unacceptable.

Color and *aroma* give important indications of the care with which the cider was made. Good bottled cider ranges in color from light amber to pale straw. Browning is undesirable because it indicates that oxidation occurred during crushing and pressing. Well-made cider has a definite, usually faint, aroma of fruit. Any foul or off-odors are the result of careless production.

Body is a measure of the blending process that most ciders undergo. Some ciders are blended by mixing together ciders produced from different batches of apples. This results in a product with a pleasant, full body. A less than satisfying product — with a too-thin body — can and often does result in cider to which excess water has been added before bottling.

Effervescence is characteristic of many bottled ciders. The bubbliness in most ciders is created just before or during bottling by artificial carbonation and is noted on the label with the wine terms *petillant*, *mousseux* or *sparkling*. Bottle-fermented cider made in the manner and style of champagne boasts natural carbonation.

As we tasted and compared bottled ciders at several different sessions, we looked for some balance, pleasant flavor, good color, and fragrant aroma. Full body and moderate effervescence were also desirable. As notes were made and discussion flourished around the table, though, the most useful rating came under the heading of *overall impression.* The best descriptions of certain ciders became more poetic than analytical.

Although there was never any unanimous agreement on a single favorite, nearly every taster left the gathering with a preference, as well as a label or two to be avoided in the future. Cider seems to fall into several different styles, some of which were more attractive to certain tasters than others. Interestingly, a cider's style is often a clue to its nationality. In general, the French ciders are light and very fruity, moderately effervescent and somewhat sweet. The English ciders are often full in body and flavor and are well-balanced. Canadian cider tends to be lighter and often sweeter than the cider from Europe. Although there are several brands of domestic cider sold in the United States, we were only able to locate one for our tastings. That bottle-fermented cider was particularly dry, fruity and flavorful, and was greatly enjoyed by all of its tasters.

FROM FRANCE

Cidre Bouché Six percent alcohol by volume; 26-ounce bottle by Trieure St. Jean, Normandy, France. This cider is light, fruity and moderately sweet. The light effervescence and clean taste make this cider a good beverage for drinking or a pleasant accompaniment to a flavorful meal.

Grand Cru Cider Less than 7 percent alcohol by volume; 22-ounce bottle by Gavrel, Ferrieres-en-Bray, Normandy, France. Sulphur dioxide added as preservative. This cider is a lighter style with balanced sweetness. A hint of apples is apparent, which makes this cider a pleasant beverage to just sit down and drink.

Purpom Less than 7 percent alcohol by volume; the largest-selling cider in France. This cider is rich in both color and flavor. It is full-bodied and leaves a pleasant, smooth aftertaste. This is a good cider to drink and serve with a full-flavored main course.

FROM ENGLAND

Merrydown Vintage Dry Cider Less than 7 percent alcohol by volume; 35.2-ounce bottle by Merrydown Wine Company Ltd., Horam

Manor, Heathfield, Sussex, England from 1977 vintage apples. This cider is nicely balanced with moderate sweetness and some acid. It is a light style that would benefit from higher carbonation, and is a pleasant beverage for drinking.

Bulmer Woodpecker Cider Almost 4 percent (3.8 percent) alcohol; 33.8-ounce bottle by H.P. Bulmer Ltd., Hereford, England. Ascorbic acid and sulphur dioxide added as preservatives. This cider is quite sweet, balanced with the sharp flavor of English cider apples. It is pleasantly bubbly and clear. This is a good cider for drinking alone, as well as with food.

Bulmer Strongbow Export Cider Five and three-quarters percent alcohol; 33.8-ounce bottle by H.P. Bulmer Ltd., Hereford, England. Ascorbic acid and sulphur dioxide added as preservatives. This is a full-bodied, well-balanced cider whose distinctively sharp flavor comes from English cider apples. It has a rich golden color, pleasant effervescence, and a strong nose. This is a beverage for full-flavored meals, as well as for drinking alone.

FROM CANADA

Grower's Dry Sparkling Cider Six percent alcohol; 12-ounce bottle by Ste. Michelle Wines, Surrey, B.C. This cider is very light in general style, and specifically in flavor, color and nose. It is somewhat balanced with acid, but shows little or no fruitiness. This beverage is dry enough to serve with food, but is a thirst-quenching refresher by itself.

Grower's Medium Sparkling Cider Six percent alcohol; 12-ounce bottle by Ste. Michelle Wines, Surrey, B.C. This cider is much like Grower's Dry, but significantly sweeter, and so is a better drink than an accompaniment to food.

Golden Valley Sparkling Apple Cider Medium Not quite 7 percent alcohol (6.7 percent); 12-ounce bottle by Brilliant Enterprises, Ltd., Westbank, B.C. This cider shows good color and pleasant effervescence. It seems sweeter than Grower's Medium and is best enjoyed as a thirst-quenching drink.

Golden Valley Sparkling Apple Cider Dry Not quite 7 percent alcohol (6.7 percent); 12-ounce bottle made by Brilliant Enterprises, Ltd. This cider is rich with good color, effervescence and mildly pleasant aftertaste. It is dry enough to enjoy with food or by itself.

FROM THE UNITED STATES

Oregon Dry Carbonated Cider Nine percent alcohol; 750-milliliter bottle by The Arterberry Ciderworks, McMinnville, Oregon. This cider is twice-fermented apple wine made in the champagne style with excellent results. Several varieties of apples are used, and the cider is rich in fruitiness and aroma. The color is light yet golden. The cider is very dry, well-balanced and a wonderful accompaniment to any fowl, pork or other meat.

CHAPTER 3

Cider
in the Kitchen

Once you have discovered the pleasure of fresh and bottled cider by the glass, it is simply a matter of time and curiosity until the satisfaction and enjoyment of cooking with cider becomes apparent. Whether fresh and very sweet or fully fermented and bone dry, cider is one of the most versatile liquids a cook can use. Since most recipes require the addition of some liquid during the cooking process, cider can be used in preparing an entire meal from the first course through dessert.

Cider is an important part of the regional cuisines of France and England. It is an essential element of such classic recipes as *tripe à la mode de Caen* from Normandy and Devon pork pie, for example. More important, though, is the general use of cider in a wide variety of meat, fowl and seafood dishes. Cider gives its own zest and flavor to many foods that are more often prepared with wine.

In order to simplify the use of cider in the kitchen, we have written recipes for three categories of cider — fresh sweet, semi-dry, or dry hard. Fresh sweet cider is recently pressed, not effervescent, and full of apple flavor. Semi-dry cider is bubbly, mildly alcoholic and fruity, but still fairly sweet. Most of the sweeter bottled ciders fall into the semi-dry category. Dry hard cider is bone dry, relatively alcoholic, not effervescent and rarely fruity when naturally fermented. Only the driest bottled ciders should be considered in this category for cooking.

Sweetness is the primary consideration for successful use of cider in cooking. The natural sugar in fresh cider averages 12 percent, which translates to two cups per gallon or four to six teaspoons per cup. Almost all bottled ciders have some sweetener added during blending. The sweetness of the cider on hand must be consistent with the desired sweetness of cider in a recipe or good food and good cider can be turned into a most unsatisfactory experiment.

Balance in the cider between sweetness and acid is also important to the cook. Most well-made cider, whether fresh or bottled, is high in acid. The sharpness of cider works to enhance the natural flavors in many foods.

Fruitiness is the third quality to consider for the most effective use of cider in the kitchen. Fresh cider often retains an apple flavor throughout the different stages of fermentation. Some bottled ciders also boast a distinctive fruitiness, which to American palates is somewhat bitter and even sour. However, many ciders, both fresh and bottled, have little apple flavor, which is a great advantage when adding cider to yeast breads, for example.

There are several different ways to prepare cider for use in the kitchen. American pioneers, especially the early colonists in New England, often boiled the fresh cider until it became a substance similar to maple syrup. Boiled cider was used to sweeten a great variety of desserts and beverages. It was the essential ingredient in a colonial favorite called boiled cider pie and a major addition to such regional specialities as Boston baked beans.

Since many hours of cooking were required to reach the proper degree of thickness, boiled cider usually lost much of its natural apple flavor and became somewhat molasses-like from prolonged exposure to heat. A more satisfactory method of concentrating cider today is by freezing.

Fresh cider is mostly water, which means that most of the sugar, acid and flavor is contained in a relatively small amount of liquid. To obtain that concentrate, remove three cups of cider from a gallon of cider and freeze the rest overnight. When the cider is thoroughly frozen, the jug can be opened and placed upside-down in a large bowl. The concentrate will thaw before the water in the cider, and most of it will be in the first five cups of melted liquid. It can be used to make several delicious desserts or can be mixed and blended with other beverages. Cider can be stored for several months in the freezer. Just be sure to thaw it completely and to shake before using so that the concentrate is blended back into the liquid.

Fresh cider can also be pasteurized to maintain a desired level of sweetness, although pasteurization is an inexact science, and results will vary depending on the cleanliness of the cider, the storage temperature, and the length of storage desired. Pour the cider into a sauce pan and heat to from 170 to 175 degrees for thirty seconds to a minute. Pour the hot cider into a bottle, cap, and invert the bottle so that every part of the container has been heated to destroy most of the organisms. Cider may be preserved at higher temperatures, but the flavor will suffer correspondingly.

Ideally, those who are just learning to cook with cider should keep a variety of bottled ciders and fresh ciders at different stages on hand. Fresh cider should be checked regularly so that the cook knows about how much sweetness, flavor and acid the cider contains. A supply of fresh cider gives the cook convenient control over the important characteristics in a fermenting gallon of fresh cider. Cider that has become too dry, for example, can be sweetened by simply adding a small amount of fresh cider.

Fresh cider not only allows the cook to control the quality and characteristics that are most important for cooking, but is generally much less expensive than bottled cider. But whether you cook with cider that is naturally fermented, or processed and bottled, we hope that you will find the results as tasty and worthwhile as we have.

U.S. METRIC EQUIVALENTS

As our U.S. kitchens are not accustomed to metric measurements, we include a basic table of equivalents for those kitchens that are.

½ teaspoon	=	2.5 milliliters
1 teaspoon	=	5 milliliters
1 tablespoon	=	15 milliliters
1 cup	=	.24 liter
1 pint	=	.47 liter
1 quart	=	.94 liter
1 gallon	=	3.8 liters
1 pound	=	453.6 grams
1 ounce	=	28.3 grams

All temperatures in this book are in degrees Fahrenheit; if you want to convert to Celsius, this is the formula:

Degrees Celsius = *Degrees Fahrenheit minus 32 × 5/9*

EQUIPMENT

The equipment required for the recipes in this book should be available in every basically well-stocked kitchen. Although it certainly can, a well-supplied kitchen need not cost a lot of money. Any pot or pan that distributes cooking heat evenly and can be cleaned easily is perfectly adequate. Some of these recipes were prepared in cast iron cookware and others in commercial-grade aluminum pots and pans. Both work very well and are highly recommended.

Although we use knives and graters for cutting vegetables, bowls and spoons for mixing, and our hands for kneading bread, those kitchens with food processors will be able, of course, to shorten the time spent on much routine kitchen work. Many cooks feel more adventuresome and creative when routine preparation is at a minimum and, since the whole idea of cooking with cider is fairly adventuresome in itself, we want to encourage whatever method is appealing. If you are using a food processor, though, your own experience or a cookbook which translates instructions written for hands into instructions for the machine will probably be necessary.

We have used a bit of shorthand in describing the equipment suggested for each recipe. It is based on the requirements of a household kitchen that is used regularly to produce meals in moderate quantity.

6-inch frying pan — small frying pan
10-inch frying pan — medium frying pan
14-inch frying pan — large frying pan
1-quart saucepan — small saucepan
2½-quart saucepan — medium saucepan
4-quart saucepan — large saucepan
5-quart casserole — small Dutch oven
8-quart casserole — large Dutch oven
12-quart casserole — stockpot
9-by-9-inch shallow baking dish — square baking pan
9-by-14-inch shallow baking dish — long baking pan
8-by-4-inch baking tin — small loaf pan
9-by-5-inch baking tin — large loaf pan

Hors d'Oeuvres

The variety of uses for cider in these hors d'oeuvres gives a good introduction to the remarkable versatility of cider in the kitchen. Fresh cider provides the sweetness in Sweet and Sour Plum Wings and a flavorful cooking liquid for Grilled Sausages. Semi-dry cider not only balances the vinegar, but gives a subtle apple flavor to an otherwise very traditional Pickled Herring. The addition of dry hard cider to Chicken Liver Paté brings all of the natural flavors in this recipe to their fullest.

Grilled Sausages

Serves 12

2 tablespoons butter
8 Polish sausages or other mildly spiced sausages, cut into
    ½-inch slices
½ teaspoon ground sage
½ cup fresh sweet cider

Melt the butter in a large frying pan over medium heat. Add the sausage slices and brown lightly on all sides. Stir the sage into the cider and then pour the liquid into the pan. Stir the sausage to cover with liquid and simmer over medium-low heat for 10 minutes, stirring occasionally.

Cool and serve with cooked mustard sauce, following.

Mustard Sauce

½ cup dry sweet mustard
½ cup cider vinegar
1 egg
1 tablespoon sugar
Dash salt
1 cup mayonnaise

Place the mustard and vinegar in a jar with a tight-fitting lid, stir well, close and let the mixture stand overnight. Combine the mustard mixture, egg, sugar and salt in the top of a double boiler and cook over medium-high heat until thickened, stirring constantly. Cool the sauce completely and then stir in the mayonnaise.

Paté

Makes 2 1-pound loaves

½ cup butter
2 medium garlic cloves, mashed
1 cup chopped scallions
8 large mushrooms, thinly sliced
2 pounds chicken livers, each piece cut in half
1½ cups dry hard cider
¼ teaspoon dried rosemary
¼ teaspoon dried dill weed
12 whole juniper berries, crushed
1 large bay leaf
2 whole cloves
1 teaspoon salt
½ teaspoon freshly ground black pepper

Melt 4 tablespoons of butter in a large frying pan. Add the garlic and sauté over medium-high heat for several minutes. Then add the scallions, mushroom and chicken livers. Reduce the heat to medium and sauté for 15 minutes, stirring occasionally.

Pour 1 cup of cider into a small saucepan and bring it to a boil. Reduce the heat to medium, add the rosemary, dill, juniper berries, bay leaf, cloves, salt and pepper, and stir well. Simmer for 15 minutes or until the liquid is reduced by half. Then pour the remaining cider into the pan and simmer for 5 more minutes. Strain the liquid to remove the whole herbs and spices and then pour it into the liver mixture. Simmer for 15 minutes over medium-low heat or until the liver is well done.

Pour the liquid from the liver mixture back into the saucepan and cook over medium heat for 20 minutes or until it measures ⅓ cup. While the liquid is reducing, put the liver mixture through the fine blades of a meat grinder or a food processor.

Melt the remaining butter in a small saucepan. Then pour the melted butter and the reduced liquid into the ground liver. Stir until the liquid and butter are thoroughly combined with the liver.

Spread the paté into two small loaf pans. Chill thoroughly before serving.

Pickled Herring

Makes 4 pints

6 fat herring, brined
Milk
3 cups cider vinegar
3 cups semi-dry cider
6 bay leaves
1 tablespoon whole allspice
2 teaspoons whole black peppercorns

1 tablespoon whole mustard seed
1 teaspoon juniper berries, crushed
¾ cup sugar
2 medium onions, thinly sliced
1 large carrot, thinly sliced

Rinse the herring well and place in a large bowl. Pour in enough milk to completely cover the fish and let stand overnight. Drain the milk from the fish, rinse them thoroughly, and cut each fish into 1-inch pieces.

Pour the vinegar and cider into a medium saucepan. Add the bay leaves, allspice, peppercorns, mustard seed, juniper berries and sugar. Bring the mixture to a boil over high heat and then reduce the heat to medium. Simmer for 10 minutes, then remove from the heat and cool. Strain to remove the whole herbs and spices and set the liquid aside. Reserve the herbs and spices.

Alternate layers of onion and herring in 4 clean pint jars, adding carrots occasionally for color. Sprinkle the spices strained from the liquid over every other layer to distribute evenly throughout each jar. Then pour the liquid into the jars until the herring and vegetables are covered. Refrigerate overnight, then serve or keep refrigerated.

Potted Cheese

Makes 4 cups

1½ pounds sharp Cheddar cheese, finely grated
1 cup sour cream
1¼ teaspoons salt
¼ teaspoon cayenne pepper
½ teaspoon mace
4 tablespoons pasteurized sweet cider
½ cup melted butter

Combine the cheese, sour cream, salt, cayenne, and mace in a large bowl and stir until thoroughly blended. Then pour in the cider and butter and stir until smooth. Pack the mixture into a 1-quart mold or several individual ramekins and refrigerate for 24 hours. To unmold, hold the mold under hot water for 10 seconds, loosen the cheese mixture by running a knife around the edges, and tap gently while holding upside-down over a serving platter.

Sweet and Sour Chicken Wings

Serves 6

½ cup milk
½ cup flour
1 teaspoon salt
½ teaspoon finely ground black pepper
2 tablespoons oil
2 tablespoons butter
12 chicken wings, tips removed and separated at the joint

Pour the milk into a small bowl. Combine the flour, salt and pepper in another small bowl and stir until mixed. Pour the oil into a medium frying pan and place over high heat until it bubbles. Add the butter to the pan and stir well, then reduce the heat to medium high.

Dip each piece of chicken in the milk, then in the flour. Place in the pan, frying for several minutes until golden. Put the fried wings in a square baking dish and bake at 350 degrees for 20 minutes or until completely cooked.

SWEET AND SOUR PLUM SAUCE

Makes 2 cups

3 tablespoons butter
2 garlic cloves, mashed
½ large green pepper, coarsely chopped
1 medium onion, coarsely chopped
1⅓ cups canned pitted plums, drained
4 tablespoons dark unsulphured molasses
1 cup fresh sweet cider
6 tablespoons cider vinegar
7 tablespoons brown sugar

Melt the butter over medium heat in a medium frying pan. Add the garlic and sauté until it is transparent. Add the green pepper and onion and sauté until the onion is golden.

Add the plums, molasses, cider, vinegar and brown sugar. Bring the mixture to a boil over high heat, then reduce heat to medium low and simmer for 15 minutes. Purée the sauce in a blender or processor and let it cool. Serve at once as a dip for the chicken wings.

Welsh Rarebit

Serves 12 as hors d'oeuvres
or 4 as an entrée

2 tablespoons butter
1 pound sharp Cheddar cheese, shredded
Dash cayenne pepper
1 teaspoon Worcestershire sauce
½ cup dry hard cider
2 eggs, beaten

Melt the butter in the top of a double boiler over gently boiling water. Then slowly add the cheese, stirring well, until the mixture is smooth. Add the pepper and Worcestershire and stir well. Pour in the cider and the eggs.

Cook over medium heat for 10 minutes or until thickened. Serve with toast cut into thin slices and lightly brushed with garlic butter.

Many traditional soup recipes are greatly enhanced by the addition of cider. It is important for the cook to evaluate carefully both the sweetness of the cider and the amount of acidity, however, before casually pouring it into a simmering pot of soup. Fresh cider that has become relatively dry, or one of the drier bottled ciders, is a delicious addition to almost any savory soup with or without meat.

Cider can be somewhat incidental, as it is in Country Borscht, or definitely essential, as it is in Onion Soup, Tomato Soup, and Corn Chowder. As an addition to a pot of stock, which will then be used in small quantities in a variety of soups, cider gives a distinctly flavorful accent.

Corn Chowder

Serves 8

½ pound ground pork sausage
1 cup dry hard cider
1 medium onion, thinly sliced
2 cubes chicken bouillon
½ cup dry milk solids
½ cup hot water
2 cans creamed corn
½ teaspoon fine ground black pepper
¼ teaspoon Tabasco Sauce
½ cup heavy cream

Place the sausage in a large frying pan and sauté over medium heat, stirring frequently for 10 minutes or until the sausage begins to brown. Pour in the cider and then add the onions and simmer over medium heat for 5 minutes.

Combine the bouillon cubes, milk solids and water in a medium bowl until cubes are dissolved. Pour this mixture into the sausage and onions, and then add the corn, pepper and Tabasco. Simmer for 10 minutes over medium-low heat. Stir in the cream and serve at once.

Country Borscht

Serves 8

6 cups stock from Cider Stew, page 88
2 cups chuck or other inexpensive cut of beef,
*   sliced into bite-size pieces*
2 teaspoons salt
2 medium onions, coarsely chopped
3 cups beets, coarsely ground in a meat grinder
*   or processor*
6 cups green cabbage, shredded
3 tablespoons cider vinegar
Sour cream

Pour the stock into a large stockpot and bring it to a boil over high heat. Add the meat, salt, onions and beets and cook for 30 minutes over medium heat or until the beets are soft. Then add the cabbage, stir well, and cook for 20 minutes or until the cabbage is completely wilted.

Pour in the vinegar and stir well. Serve at once with dollops of sour cream.

Creamy Carrot Soup

Serves 4

4 tablespoons butter
1 cup chopped onions
4 cups chopped carrots
1 cup dry hard cider
3 cups chicken stock
½ teaspoon salt
¼ teaspoon finely ground pepper
6 drops Tabasco Sauce
⅛ teaspoon nutmeg
½ cup light cream

Melt the butter in a Dutch oven. Add the onions and sauté over medium heat until they are golden. Add the carrots, cider, stock, salt, pepper, Tabasco and nutmeg and stir until thoroughly blended. Bring the liquid to a boil over high heat, then reduce the heat to medium high and cook for 20 minutes or until carrots are tender.

Remove from heat and strain. Return the liquid to the pan and simmer over low heat. Purée the carrots and onions in a blender or processor and return to the liquid. When the soup is warm, stir in the cream and serve at once.

Creamy Cauliflower Soup

Serves 4

3 tablespoons butter
1 medium onion, finely chopped
3 tablespoons flour
1 cup dry hard cider
2 cups chicken stock

¾ *teaspoon salt*
¼ *teaspoon white pepper*
¼ *teaspoon celery salt*
1 *medium head of cauliflower, broken into small flowers*
½ *cup grated white Cheddar cheese*
1½ *cups heavy cream*
¼ *teaspoon Tabasco Sauce*

Melt the butter in a stockpot over medium-high heat and add the onion. Sauté the onion until golden, then stir in the flour and cook over medium heat for 2 minutes, stirring continually. Slowly pour the cider and stock into the pot and simmer for several minutes until the mixture begins to thicken. Then add the salt, pepper and celery salt and stir well. Reduce the heat to medium low, add the cauliflower, and simmer for 20 minutes or until the cauliflower is tender.

Add the cheese and stir until it melts. Pour in the cream and Tabasco, stirring over low heat, until the soup is warmed. Serve at once.

Garden Vegetable Soup

Serves 4

BASIC STOCK
4 *quarts water*
2 *tablespoons salt*
1 *tablespoon freshly ground black pepper*
2 *bay leaves*
2 *garlic cloves, mashed*
Meaty bones from a large chicken, lamb roast or beef roast

Pour the water into a stockpot and bring to a boil over high heat. Add the salt, pepper, bay leaves and garlic, reduce the heat to simmer, and cook for 10 minutes. Add the fowl or meat, reduce the heat to medium low and simmer for several hours or until the liquid is reduced by half. Strain the liquid and reserve for soup.

SOUP

4 cups well-seasoned chicken stock or
6 cubes chicken bouillon and 4 cups water
2 cups dry hard cider
6 medium carrots, peeled and chopped into bite-size chunks
1 bunch scallions, peeled and coarsely chopped
1 small head broccoli, cut into very small flowers
1 small bunch spinach, stems removed and coarsely chopped
1 cup cooked thin egg noodles, drained
Salt and pepper

Bring the stock or water to a boil over high heat in a stockpot. If you are using water, add the bouillon and stir until the cubes are completely dissolved. Then pour in the cider, stir well, and reduce the heat to medium low.

Add the carrots, scallions and broccoli, cover the pot and simmer for 20 minutes or until the vegetables are tender. Then stir in the spinach and noodles and cook for 10 more minutes or until the spinach is completely wilted. Add salt and pepper to taste and serve very warm.

Lentil Soup

Serves 12

1½ pounds ham hocks
6 cups semi-dry cider
5 cups water
2 cups lentils

3 tablespoons butter
2 garlic cloves, mashed
1 large onion, coarsely chopped
2 cups canned tomatoes with liquid, chopped
¼ teaspoon dried oregano
¼ teaspoon dried rosemary
¼ teaspoon dried marjoram
¼ teaspoon dried sage
2 teaspoons salt
1 teaspoon black pepper
4 tablespoons molasses
2 tablespoons vinegar

Put the ham hocks, cider, water and lentils in a stockpot and bring to a boil over high heat. Cook for 10 minutes, then reduce heat to medium low.

Put the butter into a medium frying pan, add the garlic and sauté briefly over medium heat. Then add the onions and sauté until transparent. Add the tomatoes, herbs, salt and pepper and stir well. Pour in the molasses and vinegar and bring the mixture to a boil, cooking for several minutes. Remove from heat and pour over the lentil mixture. Simmer over medium-low heat for 4 hours with the pot covered. Remove the cover and simmer for an additional hour. Add the vinegar and serve at once.

Onion Soup

Serves 4 for dinner or
8 as a first course

4 tablespoons butter
3 cups thinly sliced onions
12 cups beef or chicken stock

1½ cups semi-dry cider
3 tablespoons chopped scallions
½ teaspoon freshly ground black pepper
4 thick slices French bread
½ pound Jarlsberg or Gruyère cheese, thinly sliced

Melt the butter in a medium frying pan over medium-high heat and sauté the onions until they are limp. Pour the stock into a stockpot and bring it to a boil over high heat. Reduce the heat to medium and pour in the cider. Stir well, add the onions, scallions, and pepper. Cover the pot and simmer for 40 minutes over medium-low heat.

Toast the bread and cut each piece in half. Place the bread in a small Dutch oven and pour the soup over the top. Cover the soup with cheese and place in the oven under the broiler for 3 minutes or until the cheese begins to bubble and brown.

Pumpkin Soup

Serves 4

4 small fresh pumpkins or 1 medium one
1 cup water
1 cup fresh sweet cider
2 cups chicken stock
1 cup heavy cream
¼ teaspoon nutmeg
¼ teaspoon curry powder
½ teaspoon lemon juice
Chopped parsley

Remove the seeds and stringy pulp from the pumpkins and place them in two long baking dishes with enough water to cover the bottom of the pans. Steam in a moderate oven for 20 minutes or until a spoon easily pries the flesh away from the rind. Remove the flesh from each pumpkin, carefully preserving the shells, and place in a large Dutch oven.

Pour in the water, cider and stock and bring to a boil over high heat. Reduce the heat to medium and simmer for 15 minutes. Purée the mixture in a blender or processor until it is smooth. Return to the Dutch oven and add the cream, nutmeg, and curry powder, stirring well. Then pour in the lemon juice and heat until warmed. Serve in the pumpkin shells and garnish with chopped parsley.

Sour Cherry Soup

Serves 6 for dessert

4 cups fresh or frozen pie cherries
4 cups fresh sweet cider
1¼ cups sugar
4 tablespoons cornstarch
3 tablespoons butter

Place the cherries in a large saucepan. Pour in 3½ cups cider, add the sugar and stir well. Bring to a boil over high heat, then reduce the heat to medium and cook for 15 minutes.

Stir the cornstarch into the remaining cider. Add to the cherry mixture and stir until thoroughly blended. As soon as the soup begins to thicken, remove it from the heat. Then add the butter, stir well and cool. Serve as soup or as a topping for Cottage Pudding, page 132.

Split Pea Soup

2 cups green split peas
3 cups water
1½ cups semi-dry or dry hard cider
2 medium celery stalks, finely chopped
2 medium carrots, peeled and finely chopped
1 medium onion, minced
2 teaspoons salt
½ teaspoon dried marjoram
¼ teaspoon dried rosemary
¼ teaspoon dried sage
¼ teaspoon dried oregano
2½ cups milk
2 tablespoons bacon drippings
3 strips slab bacon, cooked and crumbled
Croutons

Wash the peas thoroughly and drain well. Pour the water and cider into a large Dutch oven and bring to a boil over high heat. Add the peas, celery, carrots and onion and stir well. Sprinkle in the salt, marjoram, rosemary, sage and oregano and stir. Reduce the heat to medium low, cover the pan, and simmer the soup for 45 minutes or until the peas are very soft.

Pour the soup into a blender or processor and purée until smooth. Add the milk and bacon drippings and stir until thoroughly blended. Garnish with bacon and croutons.

Squashage Soup

Serves 8

1 cup water
1½ cups semi-dry cider
5 cups yellow summer squash, cut into
 bite-size chunks
4 tablespoons butter
¾ teaspoon freshly ground black pepper
1 teaspoon salt
¼ teaspoon ground nutmeg
6 small pork sausages
2 cups milk
½ cup chopped scallion tops

Pour the water and 1 cup of cider into a large Dutch oven and bring to a boil over high heat. Add the squash, butter, pepper, salt and nutmeg and stir well. Simmer over medium heat for 40 minutes or until the squash is soft and the liquid is thickened.

Pour the remaining cider into a small frying pan and bring it to a boil over high heat. Add the sausage, reduce the heat to medium and cook until the liquid disappears and the sausage is lightly browned. Remove the sausages from the pan and cut into thin slices. Add to squash mixture.

Pour ½ cup of milk into the squash mixture and stir well. Simmer over low heat for 10 minutes, then add the remaining milk and scallion tops and heat until warm. Serve at once.

Tomato Soup

Serves 4

¾ cup dry hard or semi-dry cider
3 cups canned peeled tomatoes, with juice
2 stalks celery, chopped
1 bunch scallions, chopped

1 teaspoon dried basil or
1 tablespoon fresh basil
½ teaspoon salt
¼ teaspoon pepper
2 garlic cloves, mashed
2 tablespoons butter
2 tablespoons flour
1 cup light cream

Pour the cider into a large Dutch oven. Add the tomatoes and juice, celery, scallions, basil, salt, pepper and garlic and stir well. Bring to a boil over high heat and then reduce the heat to medium and simmer for 20 minutes.

In a small frying pan, melt the butter over medium heat and add the flour, cooking for two minutes and stirring until smooth. Pour in the cream and stir well until mixture is smooth, cooking over low heat.

Stir cream sauce into soup. Serve with vegetable chunks or purée in a blender or processor.

Both fresh sweet and dry hard cider can be used imaginatively in a variety of salads. Almost any combination of vegetables, grains and dried beans becomes more flavorful when the legumes are cooked in dry cider and water. Such salads include Hot Lentil and Rice, both of which make an excellent main course at lunch or a tasty dinner accompaniment. Other traditional salad recipes, such as tabouleh, made with bulgur wheat, and three bean salad with kidney beans, white beans and onions, are particularly tasty when prepared with cider.

Fresh sweet cider provides an excellent base for almost any molded fruit salad. Dry cider is well suited to a flavorful combination of vegetables.

Cider is a zesty addition to several tangy salad dressings as well. It provides some acidity and sweetness in a mildly flavored Mustard Dressing, and additional sweetness in a stirred Sweet and Sour Dressing. Cider used in fresh dressings must be pasteurized if the dressing is not to be used immediately, or it will soon ferment the dressing.

Cucumber Salad

Serves 3 to 4

1 large cucumber, peeled and thinly sliced
Salt
½ cup semi-dry cider
¼ cup cider vinegar

Layer the cucumber slices in a small soup bowl. Sprinkle salt lightly between the layers. Place a matching bowl on top of the one with cucumbers and shake vigorously for two minutes.

Pour the cider and vinegar over the cucumbers, and mix with the juice that has been released by the salt and shaking.

Hot Lentil Salad

Serves 4

1 cup lentils
1 cup well-seasoned beef stock or
1 beef bouillon cube and 1 cup water
1 cup dry hard cider
1 bunch scallions, peeled and finely chopped
3 tablespoons fresh parsley, finely chopped
3 tablespoons cider vinegar
1 egg yolk, lightly beaten
½ cup sour cream

Soak the lentils for 2 hours in enough water to cover them completely. Pour the stock into a medium saucepan and then add the cider. Stir the liquid once and bring to a boil over high heat. Then add the lentils, cover the pan and reduce the heat to medium low. Simmer for 40 minutes or until the lentils are tender.

Drain the lentils, and combine them with the scallions and parsley. In a separate bowl, combine the vinegar and egg yolk and beat until thoroughly blended. Then slowly add the egg mixture to the sour cream and stir well.

Pour the dressing over the lentils and serve on a bed of fresh lettuce.

Molded Fruit Salad

Serves 6

4 cups sweet cider
2 envelopes powdered unflavored gelatin
2 tablespoons sugar
½ cup thinly sliced bananas
1 cup thinly sliced strawberries
4-ounce package cream cheese, formed into small balls

Pour 1 cup of cider into a small saucepan and sprinkle the gelatin over the top. Cook over low heat, stirring constantly, for 3 minutes or until the gelatin is completely dissolved. Pour in the sugar and stir the mixture until the sugar dissolves. Skim any foam that may have accumulated.

Pour the remaining cider into a medium bowl. Add the gelatin/cider mixture and stir well. Pour into a mold and chill until partially set.

Combine the bananas and strawberries and fold them carefully into the gelatin. Form the cream cheese into small balls using a melon baller and add them carefully to the mold. Chill the mold until firm. Unmold in warm water just before serving.

Molded Vegetable Salad

Serves 6

3½ cups fresh sweet cider
2 envelopes powdered unflavored gelatin
4 tablespoons cider vinegar
½ teaspoon salt
½ cup cooked beets, thinly sliced or grated
½ cup cooked carrots, thinly sliced or grated
½ cup celery, thinly sliced
¼ cup walnuts, finely chopped

Pour 1 cup of cider into a small saucepan and sprinkle the gelatin over the top. Cook over low heat, stirring constantly, for 3 minutes or until the gelatin is completely dissolved. Remove the mixture from the heat and skim any foam that may have accumulated.

Pour the remaining cider into a bowl. Add the vinegar and salt and stir until well blended. Then add the cider/gelatin mixture and stir well. Pour the liquid into a mold and chill until partially set.

Combine the beets, carrots, celery and walnuts and fold into the gelatin, making sure that the vegetables and nuts are completely covered with gelatin. Chill until firm and serve with homemade mayonnaise.

Rice Salad

Serves 6

2 cups steamed white or brown rice, cooked
in dry hard cider
½ cup chopped carrots
½ cup scallion tops, finely chopped
½ cup celery, chopped
2 tablespoons olive oil
1 tablespoon white wine vinegar
Salt and pepper
2 fresh tomatoes, chopped into quarters
12 cooked shrimp, shelled and cleaned

Combine the rice, carrots, scallions and celery in a large bowl. Mix the oil and vinegar well and pour over the rice and vegetables. Add salt and pepper to taste and chill for 1 hour.

Stir in the shrimp, garnish with tomato slices, and serve.

Tomato Aspic

Serves 4

1 cup tomato juice
1 stalk celery, broken into several pieces
3 tablespoons onion, coarsely chopped
Pinch paprika
½ teaspoon salt
1 teaspoon lemon juice or cider vinegar
1 small bay leaf
1 tablespoon gelatin
1 cup dry hard cider, hot, but not boiling

Pour the tomato juice into a small saucepan and add the celery, onion, paprika, salt, lemon juice or vinegar, and bay leaf. Simmer over medium heat for 5 minutes.

Dissolve the gelatin in ½ cup of cider. Strain the tomato juice mixture and add it to the cider. Stir well, then add the rest of the cider and stir again until well blended.

Pour the liquid into a mold and chill until firm.

Tomato Tomato Salad

Serves 4

2 large scallions, finely chopped
1 tablespoon sugar
½ teaspoon salt
¼ cup dry hard cider
1 teaspoon Worcestershire sauce
6 tablespoons vinegar

½ cup tomato sauce
1½ cups vegetable oil
2 large tomatoes, thinly sliced
1 medium sweet onion, thinly sliced

Put the scallions, sugar, salt, cider, Worcestershire and vinegar into a blender or processor. Blend until mixture is liquified. Pour in the tomato sauce and blend well. Then drizzle in the oil while blender or processor is running on moderate speed, until the dressing begins to thicken.

Place a layer of tomatoes in a bowl, top with a layer of onions, then tomatoes, then the rest of the onions. Pour the dressing evenly over the top. Chill for several hours before serving.

Basic Creamy French Dressing

Makes about 1 cup

4 tablespoons vinegar
2 tablespoons dry hard cider
½ teaspoon salt
1½ teaspoons sugar
¼ teaspoon dry mustard
1 egg
Dash freshly ground black pepper
¾ cup vegetable oil

Pour the vinegar and cider into a blender or processor. Then add the salt, sugar, mustard, egg and pepper. Blend at a high speed until the mixture is thoroughly combined. Then slowly add the oil in a thin stream while the blender is running at a moderate speed. Chill before using. If dressing is not used at once, pasteurize the cider before adding.

Mustard Salad Dressing

Makes 1½ cups

⅓ cup sugar
1 teaspoon dry hot mustard
½ teaspoon salt
1 teaspoon flour
1 tablespoon butter
1 egg, beaten
¼ cup dry hard cider
¼ cup cider vinegar

Put the sugar, mustard, salt, and flour in the top of a double boiler and mix well. Add the butter, egg, cider and vinegar and stir. Cook the dressing over boiling water, stirring constantly until thickened, about 5 minutes.

Reduce the heat to medium low and simmer for 10 more minutes. Chill before using and dilute in equal parts with cream, hard cider or evaporated milk. Serve on cole slaw or spring lettuce. This dressing keeps well and can be made in quantity. Do not dilute until just before serving.

Sweet and Sour Salad Dressing

Makes 1½ cups

½ cup dry hard cider
2 tablespoons cider vinegar
1 teaspoon dry mustard
½ teaspoon salt
1 teaspoon celery seed
4 tablespoons honey
1 cup vegetable oil

Pour the cider and vinegar into a blender and then add the mustard, salt and celery seed. Blend on low speed until thoroughly combined, then slowly add the honey, blending until it is completely mixed. Slowly drizzle the oil in a fine stream into the mixture until the dressing thickens. Serve on melon balls or fresh fruit salad.

Semi-dry cider, either bottled or naturally fermented, is a remarkable addition to either yeast or quick bread. The effect on yeast bread is dramatic and will be familiar to those who bake with sourdough or add beer to their bread dough. But unlike beer, cider leaves no bitter aftertaste in the finished product and unlike sourdough, it requires no maintenance of a starter.

Cider yeast combines with regular bread yeast in a way that makes the dough rise more lightly and evenly. The natural sugars in cider add some sweetness and the acids and alcohol give protection against spoilage. In addition, cider adds a slightly fruity flavor that is a tasty contribution to most whole grain and even French breads.

Cider sugars add crunchiness to the bread crust. They give the bread yeast additional food to continue working and to help keep the bread moist for an exceptional length of time.

Although the yeast bread recipes that follow are written for all-purpose flour, the unbleached "bread" flours, which contain more gluten, would be excellent in breads made with cider. The leavening action of cider is even more significant when combined with hard-to-leaven flours such as rye. It is so successful that one recipe, Fermented Rye Bread, actually requires no bread yeast at all.

Cider can be used in any bread recipe that requires milk, such as Sweet Bread, by substituting cider for the amount of liquid and adding ½ cup dry milk solids per cup of liquid into the dough. Cider should never be substituted for milk without the solids.

Dry hard cider can be a valuable addition to spicy quick breads, like Cheese and Cider Bread, but should be avoided in yeast breads because it can slow down or prevent proper fermentation of the bread yeast. Since quick breads are chemically leavened, the process is not nearly as delicate as it is when yeast is involved. Dry hard cider should only be used in flavorful breads or its sharp aftertaste will be apparent.

Sweet cider makes sweet breads, cakes, and cookies much lighter in texture than when they are made with another liquid. The cider flavor comes through as well, especially when spices and other flavorings are used with restraint.

YEAST BREADS

Cider Dough

Makes 2 large loaves

SPONGE
1 cup semi-dry cider, at room temperature
1 cup all-purpose flour

Combine the cider and flour thoroughly in a large bowl. Cover the bowl and let it stand in a warm place for 24 hours. The sponge should be very bubbly before it is used.

DOUGH
1 cup semi-dry cider, at room temperature
1 teaspoon sugar
3 teaspoons salt
Sponge
1 package (1 tablespoon) active dry yeast
¼ cup warm water
4 to 5 cups all-purpose flour
1 tablespoon oil

Add the cider, sugar, and salt to the sponge and stir until thoroughly blended. Dissolve the yeast in the water and then blend into the sponge.

Add 2 cups of flour to the mixture and beat well for 2 minutes. Then add 2 more cups of flour, one at a time, stirring well. When the dough is hard to stir and comes clean from the bowl, place it on a board that has been sprinkled with ½ cup of flour. Knead the dough 5 minutes, adding small amounts of flour to the board to prevent it from sticking.

Pour the oil into the bottom of a bowl. Put the dough in the bowl and turn until the surface is evenly coated with oil. Cover the bowl and let the dough rise in a warm place until it is doubled in bulk, usually 1½ to 2 hours.

Punch the dough down and let it rest for 15 minutes. Remove it from the bowl and knead briefly on a very lightly floured board. Then divide the dough into two equal pieces. With a rolling pin, flatten each piece into an 8-by-10-inch rectangle. Starting on the 10-inch side, roll the dough like a jelly roll, sealing the edge carefully to the rest of the roll. Tuck the ends under the loaf and pinch them shut.

Place the loaves in well-greased large loaf pans. Let the loaves rise in a warm place until the top rises just over the edge of the pan. Bake at 400 degrees for 30 to 35 minutes. Remove immediately from the pans and brush the top of each loaf with melted butter. Cover them with a clean towel and let them cool on racks.

Fermented Rye Bread

Makes 3 small loaves

SPONGE
1 cup semi-dry cider, at room temperature
1 cup medium rye flour

Mix the cider and flour thoroughly in a quart jar or small bowl. Let it stand, covered, in a warm spot for 12 to 48 hours. The sponge will be very runny and bubbly when it is ready to use.

DOUGH
2 cups semi-dry cider, room temperature
3 cups medium rye flour
Sponge
1 teaspoon salt
¼ cup molasses
2 teaspoons fennel or caraway seeds
2 cups all-purpose flour
2½ cups medium rye flour

Combine the cider and 3 cups of rye flour in a large bowl and stir until thoroughly mixed. Add the sponge and stir until blended. Let the dough stand for 8 to 12 hours, covered, in a warm place. Add the salt, molasses, and fennel or caraway seeds and mix thoroughly. Then add the all-purpose flour, one cup at a time, stirring well after each addition. Add 2 cups of rye flour, one cup at a time, stirring well after each addition. The dough should be very stiff but still quite sticky.

Place the dough on a board that has been sprinkled with the remaining rye flour. Knead thoroughly until the dough is malleable and no longer sticks to your hands. The dough will remain slightly sticky.

Divide the dough into 3 equal portions. Shape into balls and place on greased sheets. Let the loaves rise 1½ to 2 hours in a warm room or 8 hours in a refrigerator. If allowed to rise in the refrigerator, let the dough rest and come to room temperature, usually about 45 minutes, before baking. Brush the loaves with beaten egg white.

Bake at 400 degrees for 35 to 40 minutes or until the loaves sound hollow when tapped. Remove from the baking sheets, cover with a clean towel and let cool.

Oatmeal Bread

Makes 3 small loaves

2 tablespoons (2 packages) active dry yeast
¼ cup warm water
2 cups semi-dry cider, at room temperature
¼ cup honey, warmed
2 tablespoons shortening, broken into small pieces
1 tablespoon salt
4 cups all-purpose flour
2 cups uncooked rolled oats

Dissolve the yeast in warm water. Let the mixture stand for 15 minutes. Then add the cider, honey, shortening and salt and stir well. Add 2 cups of all-purpose flour and beat briskly for 5 minutes. Then add the oatmeal, one cup at a time, beating well after each addition. Add the remaining flour and stir until the dough is stiff and comes clean from the sides of the bowl.

Turn the dough onto a lightly floured board and knead for 3 minutes until it is smooth and elastic. Place the dough in an oiled bowl, turning it to coat evenly with oil. Let the dough rise, covered, in a warm place until it is double in size, usually about 1 hour.

Punch the dough down and let it rest for a few minutes. Shape into 3 equal round loaves. Place loaves on greased baking sheets and let them rise until they are double, usually about 45 minutes. Brush each loaf with egg white. Bake at 375 degrees for 45 to 50 minutes or until the loaves sound hollow when tapped. Remove from baking sheets and cool on racks.

Sour Rye Bread

Makes 2 large loaves

1 package (1 tablespoon) active dry yeast
¼ cup warm water
1 tablespoon sugar
2 cups all-purpose flour
5 cups rye flour
½ cup whole wheat flour
1 cup buttermilk
¾ cup dry hard cider
2 teaspoons salt
3 tablespoons caraway seeds

Dissolve the yeast in the water and then stir in the sugar. Let the mixture stand for 15 minutes. Stir in ½ cup of all-purpose flour and set aside until bubbles form. Then stir in the remaining all-purpose flour, rye flour and whole wheat flour, one cup at a time. Pour in the buttermilk and cider as needed to moisten the dough while adding the flour. Then add the salt and caraway seeds and combine thoroughly.

Place the dough on a lightly floured board and knead for 10 minutes or until the dough is very smooth and elastic. Place the dough in an oiled bowl, turning it to coat evenly with oil. Let the dough rise, covered, in a warm place until it is double in size, usually about 1½ hours.

Punch the dough down and let it rest for a few minutes. Then shape it into two loaves and place them in two large loaf pans. Let them rise until they are doubled, usually about 1½ hours. Bake at 400 degrees for 15 minutes and then reduce the heat to 350 degrees and bake for 1¼ hours, or until the loaves are evenly browned.

Standby Yeast Rolls

Makes 48 3-inch rolls

2 packages (2 tablespoons) active dry yeast
2½ cups semi-dry cider, at room temperature
1 cup butter, cut into small pieces
¼ cup sugar or honey
1 tablespoon salt
2 eggs
7½ to 8½ cups all-purpose flour

Dissolve the yeast in 1½ cups cider. Let the mixture stand for 15 minutes. Beat the butter, sugar or honey, and salt until light. Add the eggs to the butter mixture, one at a time, and beat the mixture well after each addition. Pour in the yeast and stir well. Add 4 cups of flour, a cup at a time, beating thoroughly after each addition. Beat for 1 minute. Then stir in the remaining cider.

Gradually beat in enough of the remaining flour, a cup at a time, until a soft dough is formed. Put the dough in an oiled bowl, brush it lightly with more oil, and refrigerate for at least 8 hours or up to 5 days.

To use the dough, punch it down and divide into 4 equal parts. Use one portion at a time, returning the rest to the refrigerator. Divide a portion into 12 pieces. Shape into ovals, place them almost touching in a greased long baking pan, cover, and let them rise for 2 hours. Brush the tops with melted butter and bake at 375 degrees for 15 to 18 minutes. Remove from pan and let cool on a rack.

Sticky Buns

Makes 12 buns

1 portion Standby Yeast Rolls dough
¼ cup butter
¼ cup brown sugar

1 tablespoon light corn syrup
⅓ cup chopped walnuts or pecans
¼ cup sugar
1 tablespoon ground cinnamon
Pinch mace or nutmeg

Combine the butter, brown sugar and corn syrup in a small saucepan over low heat. When butter is melted, stir in the nuts. Spoon the mixture equally into the bottoms of 12 greased muffin cups.

Roll out 1 portion of the refrigerated dough into a 10-by-12-inch rectangle. Brush the dough with melted butter and sprinkle it with a mixture of sugar, cinnamon, and mace or nutmeg. Begin at the smaller end and roll the dough like a jelly roll, pinching the edges to seal. Cut the roll into 12 even slices. Place one slice in each muffin cup, cover the pan and let the buns rise in a warm place for 2 to 2½ hours. Bake at 375 degrees for 20 to 25 minutes. When the rolls are done, immediately invert the pan onto a serving dish, as syrup will harden as it cools.

Swedish Limpa Bread

Makes 2 round loaves

1½ cups dry hard cider
2 tablespoons brown sugar
2 tablespoons oil
3 tablespoons molasses
¼ teaspoon anise seed
1 package (1 tablespoon) active dry yeast
¾ cup warm water
3½ cups all-purpose flour
2¼ cups rye flour
1 tablespoon salt
2 teaspoons grated orange rind
1 teaspoon cornstarch

Pour 1 cup of the cider into a small saucepan and bring it to a boil over high heat. Add the brown sugar, oil, molasses and anise seed and reduce the heat to low. Simmer the mixture for 5 minutes, then remove from the heat and cool.

Soften the yeast in the water in a large bowl. Pour in the cider mixture and add the all-purpose flour, stirring well until smooth. Cover with a towel and let the soft dough rise in a warm place until it is doubled, usually about 30 minutes. Punch the dough down and gradually add the rye flour, blending until the dough is smooth. Add the salt and orange rind until well combined. Cover the dough and let it rise in a warm place until it is doubled, usually about 45 minutes.

Turn the dough onto a lightly floured board and knead until it is smooth. Divide into two equal pieces and form into round loaves. Place the loaves in two well-greased pie plates. Score the top with several cuts.

Pour the remaining cider into a small saucepan and stir in the cornstarch, cooking over low heat until slightly thickened. Cool and brush the top of each loaf with some of this glaze. Cover the loaves with a clean towel and let them rise in a warm place until they are doubled, usually about 45 minutes. Brush with remaining glaze and bake in a 350 degree oven for 50 minutes or until browned. Remove from pans and cool on racks.

Sweet Bread

Makes 2 large loaves

2 packages (2 tablespoons) active dry yeast
½ cup warm water
1½ cups semi-dry cider, at room temperature
¼ cup sugar
1 tablespoon salt
½ cup dry milk solids
5-6 cups all-purpose flour (2 cups whole wheat may
    be substituted for 2 cups all-purpose)

Dissolve the yeast in warm water. Let it stand until it bubbles, about 15 minutes. Pour the cider into the yeast mixture, then stir in the sugar, salt and dry milk solids. Add 2 cups of flour and beat vigorously for 3 minutes. Add 2 more cups of flour, either all-purpose or whole wheat, one cup at a time and beat the dough well after each addition.

Add 1 more cup of flour and stir until the dough is very stiff. Place the dough on a board that has been sprinkled with ½ cup of flour. Knead the dough for 5 minutes, until it is elastic and blistered on the surface.

Place the dough in an oiled bowl, turning so that the surface is evenly coated. Let the dough rise until doubled, about 1½ hours. Divide the dough into two equal portions and roll each into an 8-by-10-inch rectangle. Beginning with the larger side, roll the dough like a jelly roll, tucking the ends and pinching the edge to seal. Place the loaves seam side down in two large loaf pans. Let rise, covered, until loaves are doubled, usually about 1 hour. Bake at 350 degrees for 35 to 40 minutes. Remove from pans and cool on racks.

The basic Sweet Bread recipe can be used for Stollen or Spice Sweet Bread.

Stollen

After the first 2 cups of flour are added in the basic recipe, add ¾ cup chopped candied fruit and ¾ cup chopped nuts. Then stir in ½ cup butter, cut into very small pieces. Continue the recipe as indicated.

When shaping the stollen, make a circle 8 inches in diameter. Then make a crease in the dough that is slightly off-center on the circle, and fold the dough over itself. Let the dough rise in a warm place. When it is baked, brush the top with melted butter and sift powdered sugar over the top.

Spice Sweet Bread

Follow the basic recipe for Sweet Bread. Brush the rolled out rectangles with melted butter. Sprinkle evenly with spiced sugar, roll up like a jelly roll, and bake as for Sweet Bread.

SPICED SUGAR

For 2 loaves

¼ cup sugar
1 teaspoon cardamom seeds, finely ground
1 tablespoon cinnamon
½ teaspoon nutmeg
½ teaspoon powdered orange peel

Combine the sugar and spices and stir until well mixed.

QUICK BREADS

Apple Nut Bread

Makes 1 loaf

2 cups all-purpose flour
1 teaspoon baking powder
1 teaspoon baking soda
1 teaspoon salt
4 tablespoons butter, softened
¾ cup sugar
2 eggs, well beaten
1 cup grated apple
1 tablespoon grated lemon peel
½ cup chopped walnuts
3 tablespoons fresh sweet cider

Combine the flour, baking powder, baking soda and salt and stir until well mixed. In a separate bowl, cream the butter, sugar and eggs until smooth. Stir in the apple, lemon peel and walnuts and then add the flour mixture. Pour in the cider and beat well, until the dough is thoroughly blended. Bake at 350 degrees in a well-greased small loaf pan for 50 minutes or until a tester inserted in the center comes out clean. Cool before slicing.

Cheese and Cider Bread

Makes 1 loaf

2 cups all-purpose flour
¼ cup sugar
½ teaspoon salt
2 teaspoons baking powder
2 tablespoons minced onion
¼ teaspoon ground thyme
½ teaspoon ground parsley
¼ cup melted butter
¼ cup dry hard cider
2 large eggs, slightly beaten
¼ cup milk
¼ cup grated sharp Cheddar cheese

Sift the flour, sugar, salt and baking powder together. Stir in the onion, thyme and parsley. Combine the butter, cider, eggs and milk in a separate bowl and stir well. Pour the cider mixture into the flour and stir until smooth.

Pour the batter into a greased 8-inch pie pan and sprinkle the cheese over the top. Bake at 400 degrees for 20 to 25 minutes. Serve warm.

Cornbread

1 egg, well beaten
½ cup fresh sweet cider
½ cup milk
2 tablespoons honey
⅔ cup yellow cornmeal
¾ cup all-purpose flour
½ cup dry milk solids
1 tablespoon baking powder
1 teaspoon salt
¼ cup oil

To the beaten egg, add the cider, milk and honey and stir well. Combine the cornmeal, flour, milk solids, baking powder and salt and stir until thoroughly mixed. Add the cider mixture to the flour mixture and stir well. Then pour in the oil and beat until smooth.

Pour the batter into a square baking pan. Bake at 425 degrees for 20 minutes.

Refrigerator Bran Muffins

Makes 50 3-inch muffins

2 cups fresh sweet cider
2 cups processed bran buds
1 cup shortening
1 cup sugar
4 well-beaten eggs
4 cups ready-to-eat bran cereal
4 cups buttermilk

5 cups flour
5 teaspoons baking soda
1 teaspoon salt

Pour the cider into a medium saucepan and bring it to a boil over high heat. Pour in the bran buds and stir well. Let the cider mixture stand for several minutes.

Combine the shortening, sugar and eggs and beat well. Then stir in the bran cereal. Pour in the buttermilk and stir well, then add the flour, baking soda and salt. Beat the batter until it is thoroughly blended.

Add the cider and bran buds and stir the batter until well blended. Drop several teaspoonsful of batter into each greased muffin cup. Bake at 400 degrees for 15 minutes or until the center of each muffin is done.

The batter can be stored in the refrigerator for up to 6 weeks and used as needed. Fruit and nuts, such as raisins, cranberries, bananas, and walnuts, can be finely chopped, tossed with a little flour, and added for variety.

Fried Breakfast Toast

Serves 2

4 slices whole-grain bread
1 cup dry hard cider
2 tablespoons sugar
2 egg yolks
½ cup warm milk
3 tablespoons butter

Trim the bread and cut each piece in half. Combine the cider and sugar and soak the bread in the cider for 5 minutes. Drain excess liquid. Beat the egg yolks and milk together and dip the bread in the mixture.

Melt the butter in a small frying pan over medium-high heat. Brown the bread lightly on both sides and serve hot with powdered sugar.

Pancakes

Makes 8 6-inch pancakes

2 cups all-purpose flour
4 teaspoons baking powder
½ teaspoon baking soda
½ teaspoon salt
2 tablespoons sugar
⅓ cup dry milk solids
2 eggs, separated
4 tablespoons melted butter
1 to 1½ cups semi-dry cider

Combine the flour, baking powder, baking soda, salt, sugar and milk solids in a large bowl and stir until thoroughly mixed. Beat the egg whites until very stiff. In a separate bowl, beat the egg yolks until they are lemon-colored. Then stir the butter and cider into the yolks and beat well. Pour the cider mixture into the flour mixture and stir until smooth. If the batter seems too thick add more cider. Then carefully fold in the beaten egg whites.

Place a small amount of butter on a griddle or in a large frying pan and set over medium heat until the surface makes a drop of water sizzle. Then pour the batter on the griddle and cook until the pancake is lightly browned. Turn it over and brown the other side.

Generally speaking, the drier the cider, the better the results will be when delicately-flavored seafood is prepared. Salmon is a notable exception to that rule because the meatiness and natural sweetness of its pink flesh can handle additional sweetness from semi-dry cider.

Local cider is traditionally added to almost every seafood dish that is prepared in coastal Normandy and Brittany. After months of adding dry cider to poaching liquids, bastes, and sauces in the coastal Pacific Northwest, we certainly understand why. Dry cider is a superb substitute for dry white wine in almost any recipe. Like a good wine, it subtly enhances the natural flavors of the seafood while adding its own special dimension.

Barbecued Salmon

Serves 6

½ cup butter
2 cups dry hard cider
2 garlic cloves, mashed
4-to-5-pound salmon, cut into 6 fillets

Melt the butter in a small saucepan over medium heat. Pour in the cider, add the garlic and stir well. Reduce the heat to low and simmer for 1 hour or until the liquid is reduced by half.

Brush the salmon with the cider baste on both sides. Place the fish on a rack and cook over charcoal or wood coals, or under the broiler in the oven. Cook the fish for 10 minutes on each side, or until the center of the fillet flakes when it is touched with a fork.

There will be enough basting liquid to repeat the recipe 2 or 3 times, but to make it in smaller quantity is impractical.

Broiled Oysters

Serves 3 to 4

¼ cup melted butter
2 tablespoons dry hard cider
½ teaspoon fresh lemon juice
¼ teaspoon dried dill weed
4 drops Tabasco Sauce
12 medium oysters, preferably on the half shell
¼ teaspoon white pepper
¼ teaspoon salt
3 tablespoons finely grated fresh Parmesan cheese
1 tablespoon flour

Pour the butter, cider and lemon juice into a small saucepan and bring to a boil over high heat. Remove from the heat at once and add the dill and Tabasco, stirring well.

Arrange the oysters on their half shells in two long baking pans or in a square baking pan if they are without shells. Spoon the sauce evenly over the oysters and then sprinkle them lightly with salt and pepper. Sprinkle the cheese evenly over the top and dust lightly with flour.

Place the oysters in the oven under the broiler for 10 minutes or until the tops are lightly browned.

Fruits of the Sea

Serves 6

6 cups fumet
20 medium prawns
12 small scallops, cleaned
30 butter or little neck clams, thoroughly rinsed
1 pound black cod, cut into 4 pieces
1 pound sole or other firm white fish,
    cut into 4 pieces

FUMET

Makes about 2 quarts

6 pounds bones and trimmings from
    any white-fleshed fish
8 cups water
3½ cups dry hard cider
2 large onions, sliced
2 large carrots, sliced
2 large stalks celery, sliced
2 tablespoons salt
1 teaspoon freshly ground black pepper
½ teaspoon dried thyme
12 juniper berries, crushed
1 large bay leaf

Rinse the fish bones and trimmings thoroughly and chop them into 4-inch pieces. Pour the water and cider into a stockpot, then add the fish, onions, carrots and celery. Bring the liquid to a boil over high heat and add the salt, pepper, thyme, juniper berries and bay leaf. Reduce the heat to medium low and cover the pot. Simmer for 30 minutes. Strain the liquid and reserve.

Pour 6 cups of fumet into a stockpot and bring it to a boil over high heat. Add the prawns, return the liquid to a boil, and cook the prawns for 3 minutes. Remove the prawns from the liquid with a slotted spoon, and set aside to shell when they are cool.

Cut each scallop in half and add to the stock. Cook for 7 minutes or until completely cooked. Remove from the liquid with a slotted spoon and place with the prawns.

Put the clams in the pot. Return the stock to a boil, cover the pot, and steam for 15 minutes or until the clams are open. (Discard any that don't open.) Remove the clams with a slotted spoon and place with the prawns and scallops.

Place the cod in the pot. Simmer over medium heat for 7 minutes or until it flakes when touched with a fork. Remove from the stock with a slotted spoon and add the sole, simmering for 3 minutes or until it flakes when touched with a fork. Remove and place with the other seafood. Any excess fumet can be refrigerated or frozen for later use.

SAUCE
2 cups fumet
2 tablespoons butter
2 tablespoons lemon juice
2 tablespoons cornstarch
¼ cup water

Pour the fumet into a small saucepan, add the butter and lemon juice and bring the liquid to a boil over high heat. Combine the cornstarch and water in a separate bowl until smooth and then slowly add to the liquid. Simmer over medium-low heat, stirring continually, until the sauce thickens.

Pour the sauce over the prawns, scallops and fish. Serve with individual dishes of melted butter in which to dip the clams.

Mushroom Salmon Bake

Serves 4 to 6

12 small mushrooms, rinsed and thinly sliced
3 tablespoons butter
5 small zucchini, thinly sliced

2 cups sour cream, at room temperature
¾ cup dry hard cider
½ teaspoon dried dill weed
½ teaspoon salt
½ teaspoon black pepper
2 pounds salmon fillets

Lightly sauté the mushrooms in the butter in a medium frying pan over medium heat for 5 minutes. Remove the mushrooms from the pan and add the zucchini, sautéing over medium-low heat for 5 minutes.

Combine the sour cream, cider, dill, salt and pepper until well blended. Place the salmon in a large baking pan, cover with the vegetables, and pour the sauce over the top. Bake at 400 degrees for 20 minutes.

Mussels Mariniere

Serves 4

4 dozen small mussels, cleaned
4 small leeks, chopped into ½-inch pieces
½ cup chopped fresh parsley
4 garlic cloves, minced
1½ cups dry hard cider
Freshly ground black pepper

Place the mussels in a large Dutch oven and add the leeks, parsley and garlic. Pour in the cider, cover the pot, and steam over medium heat for 5 minutes or until the mussels open. (Discard any that don't open.) Remove the meat from the shells, strain the liquid, and add pepper to taste. Return the mussels to the liquid and serve.

Poached Salmon

Serves 6

6 quarts water
4 cups semi-dry cider
1 large orange, sliced
1 large onion, sliced
1 large lemon, sliced
4 sprigs fresh parsley
4 celery tops
½ teaspoon ground sage
½ teaspoon dried dill weed
½ teaspoon ground tarragon
5-to-6-pound salmon

Pour the water and cider into a fish poacher, or any pan with a tight-fitting lid that is big enough to hold a 5-pound fish, and bring to a boil over high heat. Add the fruit, vegetables and herbs and stir well. Reduce the heat to medium low and simmer the liquid for 30 minutes.

Place the fish on the poacher's rack or wrap in cheesecloth if using another pan. Lower the fish into the liquid, then add enough water to cover the fish. Simmer in hot but not boiling liquid for 25 to 30 minutes or about 5 minutes per pound of fish.

When the fish flakes at the backbone when touched with a fork, remove it from the poaching liquid and let it rest for 10 minutes before serving.

Prawn Sauté

Serves 4

3 tablespoons butter
2 medium onions, diced
1 pound small mushrooms, thinly sliced

½ cup semi-dry cider
¼ cup grated or flaked coconut
24 medium prawns, shelled and cleaned
3 small scallions, finely chopped

Melt the butter over medium-low heat in a large frying pan. Add the onions and mushrooms and sauté for 5 minutes or until the onion is transparent. Then pour in the cider, add the coconut, stir the mixture well and simmer for 5 minutes. Add the prawns and cook for 3 minutes, stirring constantly and taking care not to overcook. Serve over rice and garnish with scallions.

Sweet Snapper

Serves 4

1 cup fresh sweet cider
½ teaspoon whole fennel seeds, crushed
½ teaspoon ground coriander seeds
½ teaspoon grated fresh ginger
2 pounds red snapper fillets

Pour the cider into a medium frying pan and bring it to a boil over high heat. Add the fennel, coriander and ginger and reduce the heat to medium low. Simmer the liquid for 5 minutes and then place the fillets in the pan. Be sure the fish is covered with liquid; add more cider if necessary. Simmer for 15 minutes or until the center of each fillet flakes when touched with a fork. Serve at once.

Trout in Cider

5 tablespoons butter
½ cup chopped scallions
2 whole medium trout, cleaned
½ cup dry hard cider
½ cup fish stock (see Fumet, page 73)
¼ teaspoon salt
¼ teaspoon white pepper
Flour
½ cup heavy cream
2 tablespoons chopped parsley

Melt the butter in a large frying pan over medium-high heat. Add the scallions and the trout and cook for 5 minutes, turning the trout once.

Pour the cider and stock into the pan, sprinkle the salt and pepper evenly over the top and simmer over medium heat for 10 minutes, carefully turning the trout once again. Remove the trout from the pan and place it on a platter in a warm oven. Return the pan to the heat.

Shake enough flour into the liquid to thicken it slightly. Then add the cream and simmer over medium-low heat for 3 minutes. Pour the sauce over the trout, garnish with parsley and serve at once.

Fowl

As with seafood, most chicken, turkey, and wildfowl are best cooked with dry sharp cider. Sweeter ciders should be reserved for sauces, such as the honey sauce in Cider-Glazed Game Hens or Sweet and Sour Chicken. Dry cider is always an excellent baste for any fowl cooked by roasting, such as Roast Turkey. It not only adds necessary moisture to the bird, but browns and adds crispness to the skin.

Ciderbaked Chicken

Serves 3 to 4

2½-to-3½-pound chicken
1 medium onion, coarsely chopped
1 medium apple, cored and chopped into small cubes
¾ cup semi-dry cider
½ teaspoon salt
½ teaspoon freshly ground black pepper
½ teaspoon dried whole rosemary, lightly crushed

Wash the chicken in warm water and pat dry. Place the chicken in a small Dutch oven and fill the center cavity with the apples and onions. Pour the cider over the top of the chicken and then sprinkle salt, pepper and rosemary evenly over the entire bird.

Cover and bake at 350 degrees for 50 minutes or until a leg can be easily separated at the joint. Remove the cover and bake for 10 more minutes or until the skin is evenly browned.

Add flour to the pan drippings to thicken and use as gravy.

Parsley Chicken

Serves 3 to 4

2½-to-3½-pound chicken, cut into serving pieces
⅔ cup dry hard cider
1 tablespoon cider vinegar
4 large sprigs fresh parsley, finely chopped
3 garlic cloves, crushed
⅓ cup heavy cream
Salt and pepper to taste

Wash the pieces of chicken and pat dry. Pour the cider and vinegar into the bottom of a long baking pan. Combine the parsley and garlic and put half of the amount in the pan. Then place the chicken in the pan and sprinkle the remaining parsley over the top. Cover the pan with aluminum foil, sealing the edges, and bake at 375 degrees for 40 minutes, turning the pieces of chicken once or twice. Remove the foil for the last 5 minutes of cooking.

Remove the chicken from the pan, pour in the cream and stir to deglaze the pan juices. Simmer over low heat until the sauce begins to thicken. Add salt and pepper to taste and serve over the chicken or accompanying rice.

Soybaked Chicken

Serves 6 to 8

2 3-to-4-pound chickens, cut into serving pieces
2 cups semi-dry cider
½ cup soy sauce
4 garlic cloves, mashed
2 small onions, quartered
¼ teaspoon pepper
½-inch piece fresh ginger, peeled and thinly sliced
⅛ teaspoon ground oregano
⅛ teaspoon ground marjoram
1 teaspoon lemon juice
1 teaspoon salt

Arrange the chicken pieces in a large Dutch oven. Combine the cider and soy and stir well. Then add the garlic, onion, pepper, ginger, oregano, marjoram, lemon juice and salt. Pour the liquid mixture over the chicken and cover the pot.

Bake at 375 degrees for 1 hour or until the chicken pulls easily from the bone. Serve over rice.

Sweet and Sour Chicken

Serves 4

SAUCE
½ cup cider vinegar
½ cup fresh sweet cider
½ cup sugar
2 teaspoons soy sauce
2 teaspoons cornstarch

1 cup uncooked white rice
2 cups water
4 tablespoons oil
3-to-4-pound chicken, boned and cut into 1½-inch pieces
1 tablespoon grated fresh ginger
2 large garlic cloves, peeled and finely chopped
1 large onion, chopped into ½-inch pieces
1 stalk broccoli, chopped into 1-inch pieces
1 small green pepper, chopped into 1-inch pieces
¼ cup canned pineapple chunks
10 cherry tomatoes, each cut in half

Combine the vinegar and cider in a small saucepan and bring to a boil over high heat. Reduce the heat to medium low, add the sugar, and simmer for 5 minutes, stirring frequently, until the sugar is dissolved. Pour in the soy sauce and stir. Then slowly add the cornstarch, stirring well, until the sauce thickens sufficiently to coat a spoon. Keep the sauce warm while assembling the rest of the recipe and stir it occasionally.

Bring the water to a boil over high heat in a medium saucepan. Add the rice, reduce the heat to low and cover. Cook for 20 minutes or until the liquid is completely absorbed and the rice is soft.

Pour the oil into a large frying pan, add the ginger and garlic and cook over high heat until the garlic is lightly browned. Then place the chicken in the pan and cook until golden, turning each piece frequently. Remove the chicken from the pan when it is brown and pour off all but two tablespoons of oil.

Reheat the oil and add the onion, broccoli and green pepper. Stir the vegetables constantly until they are evenly coated with oil and cook them for several minutes until they are barely tender. Return the chicken to the pan and combine with the vegetables, then add the pineapple and tomatoes. Cook for several more minutes, removing from the heat when the tomatoes begin to wilt.

Spoon the chicken and vegetables over the rice and pour sauce evenly over the top.

Cider-Glazed Game Hens

Serves 4

4 tablespoons butter
2 medium onions, finely chopped
4 medium stalks of celery, finely chopped
¼ teaspoon ground marjoram
¼ teaspoon ground sage
¼ teaspoon ground thyme
Pinch mace
4 small tart apples, peeled, cored and cubed
½ cup chicken stock
Salt and freshly ground black pepper to taste
4 10-ounce Cornish game hens

SAUCE
1 cup fresh sweet cider
½ cup honey
2 tablespoons flour
½ cup heavy cream
2 tablespoons dry sherry

Melt the butter in a large frying pan. Add the onions and celery and sauté over medium-high heat until limp. Sprinkle in the marjoram, sage and thyme and stir well. Then continue cooking over medium heat until the onions are golden. Add the apples, stock, salt and pepper, stir well, and remove from the heat.

Fill the cavity of each bird with the stuffing and secure with poultry pins. Bake at 400 degrees for 50 minutes or until a leg can be easily separated at the joint, basting occasionally with pan drippings.

Combine the cider and honey in a small saucepan over medium heat. Add the flour and cook for several minutes, stirring constantly until the mixture thickens. Remove from the heat and stir in the cream and sherry. Keep warm over low heat until the hens are removed from the oven. Pour the sauce evenly over each bird and serve at once.

Apple Pheasant

Serves 3 to 4

2½-to-3-pound pheasant, cleaned and cut into serving pieces
1 teaspoon salt
¼ teaspoon freshly ground black pepper
½ cup flour
4 slices bacon
3 tablespoons butter
1 large onion, coarsely chopped
½ pound mushrooms, thinly sliced
½ cup dry hard cider
1 garlic clove, mashed
3 medium apples, cored and chopped into small cubes
¼ cup Calvados or applejack
1 cup sour cream, at room temperature
½ cup chicken stock

Sprinkle the pheasant with salt and pepper, then dredge each piece in flour and set aside. Cook the bacon over medium-high heat in a large frying pan. Remove from the pan when cooked and crumble for garnish. Pour all but 1 tablespoon of fat from the frying pan and add the butter. Return the pan to medium-high heat, melt the butter, and place pheasant in the pan to brown lightly on all sides. Remove the pheasant and place in a warm oven, covering with a damp cloth.

Place the onion and mushrooms in the frying pan and sauté over medium heat for 5 minutes or until the onions are golden. Then pour in the cider and add the garlic. Stir the contents of the pan and then return the pheasant. Cook over medium heat for 10 minutes. Add a few chopped apples and continue cooking for 10 more minutes. Then add the remainder of the apples, reduce the heat to medium low and simmer for 5 minutes. If the pheasant is pink at the bone, continue cooking for 10 more minutes.

Combine the Calvados, sour cream, chicken stock and 1 tablespoon of flour in a small saucepan. Simmer over low heat for 5 minutes, stirring constantly. Pour the sauce over the pheasant and serve at once with rice or noodles.

Pheasant Kiteen

Serves 4 to 5

4 tablespoons butter
4 tablespoons oil
1 pound fresh matsutake or other flavorful mushroom,
  thinly sliced
2 shallot cloves, finely chopped
¾ cup dry hard cider
1 teaspoon dried basil
¼ teaspoon salt
Dash black pepper
Pinch cayenne pepper
4 medium onions, diced
2 2½-to-3-pound pheasants, cleaned, boned and cut into
  small cubes

Put the butter and oil into a large frying pan and stir over high heat. Reduce the heat to medium and add the mushrooms and onions. Sauté for 10 minutes and then add the shallots. Sauté for several more minutes or until shallots are transparent.

Pour in the cider and sprinkle the basil, salt, pepper and cayenne evenly over the top. Return the heat to medium high and add the pheasant. Sauté for 15 minutes or until the pheasant is lightly browned on all sides, stirring constantly. Serve with rice.

Roast Turkey

Serves 20 +

15-to-18-pound turkey
1 garlic clove, mashed
1½ pounds butter
2 teaspoons ground thyme

3 teaspoons salt
1 teaspoon ground pepper
¼ teaspoon Tabasco Sauce
2 teaspoons whole celery seed
1 teaspoon dried oregano
½ teaspoon ground mace
4 large apples, cored and quartered
4 large onions, quartered
2 teaspoons ground sage
2 teaspoons salt
3 cups semi-dry cider

Rub the turkey both inside and out with salt and pepper. Put the butter and garlic in a large frying pan and place over medium-high heat. When butter melts, add the thyme, salt, pepper, Tabasco, celery seed, oregano and mace. Reduce heat to medium low and simmer for 10 minutes.

Fold a cotton knit cloth in half to measure about 15 by 18 inches. A dishtowel or T-shirt will do. Put it in the pan and let it soak up the butter and seasonings for several minutes.

Combine the apples, onions, sage and salt and stuff the center cavity of the turkey with this mixture. Secure the openings with poultry pins and place breast side down in a large roasting pan.

Drape the cloth over the turkey, covering as much of the surface as possible. Roast the bird at 350 degrees for 12 minutes per pound. Pour the cider into the frying pan that held the seasoned butter. Bring it to a boil over medium-high heat and then remove from the heat. Use the cider to baste the turkey every 15 minutes. When the cider is used up, baste with pan drippings. Turn the turkey breast side up after 90 minutes of roasting, using heavy rubber gloves to protect your hands from the heat.

Throw the stuffing — and the cloth — away when the bird is fully cooked. Serve with all the trimmings.

Nowhere is cider more useful than in the preparation of beef, lamb and pork. The fruitiness of the cider combines wonderfully with almost any meat, whether it is Cider Stew with beef, Devon Pork Pie or Ginger Lamb. The addition of cider also helps break down tough fibers in less expensive cuts of meat, as does wine, during a slow cooking procedure.

Most beef and lamb dishes are best when dry cider is used. Semi-dry and even sweet cider can be used, however, with most cuts of pork, whether fresh or already cooked. Dry cider almost always makes a flavorful gravy of pan drippings after cooking, or it can be added to the pan after the meat is removed to deglaze the juices.

Dry cider is an excellent addition in the preparation of Sautéed Sweetbreads, Tongue in Aspic and other specialty meats. Of course, cider is the traditional liquid used in *Tripe à la Mode de Caen*.

Beef and Broccoli Ragout

Serves 4

2 tablespoons oil
2 garlic cloves, crushed
1½ teaspoons salt
1½ pounds chuck steak, cut into bite-size cubes
2 tablespoons flour
1 cup dry hard cider

1½ *cups beef bouillon*
2 *bay leaves*
½ *teaspoon crushed whole thyme*
½ *teaspoon freshly ground black pepper*
4 *leeks, thinly sliced* or
8 *whole small onions, peeled*
5 *carrots, quartered lengthwise*
½ *pound mushrooms, thinly sliced*
2½ *cups sliced broccoli stalks and flowers*
¼ *cup chopped fresh parsley*

Pour the oil into a Dutch oven and place over high heat. Add the garlic and salt and sauté briefly. Dredge the beef in the flour and brown on all sides. Pour in the cider and bouillon and stir, then add the bay leaves, thyme and pepper. Stir the mixture well and add the leeks or onions, mushrooms and carrots. Bring to a boil, then reduce the heat to medium low. Simmer with the pot covered for 20 minutes.

Add the broccoli and parsley and simmer for 15 minutes or until the broccoli is tender.

Cider Stew

Serves 4

2 *tablespoons butter*
3 *pounds stewing beef or short ribs, or combination*
2 *cups dry hard cider*
2 *cups water*
2 *large garlic cloves, mashed*
2 *medium onions, quartered*
¼ *teaspoon ground thyme*
Salt and pepper to taste

Place the butter in a medium frying pan and melt over high heat. Add the beef and brown quickly on all sides. Pour the cider and water into a small Dutch oven. Bring the liquid to a boil over high heat and add the garlic, onions, thyme, salt and pepper. Reduce the heat to medium low and add the meat. Simmer for 2 hours until the meat is very tender.

Cook vegetables — such as carrots, turnips and potatoes — separately and add to the stew just before serving.

Beef Stroganoff

Serves 4

3 tablespoons butter
1 tablespoon flour
1 cup dry hard cider
1½ pounds round steak, cut into small cubes
1 large onion, thinly sliced
½ teaspoon dried dill weed
3 tablespoons sour cream, at room temperature

Melt 2 tablespoons of butter in a large frying pan over medium heat. Stir in the flour and cook for 2 minutes, stirring constantly. Then pour in the cider and simmer for 5 minutes, stirring occasionally, until the sauce begins to thicken. Keep the sauce warm over low heat.

In a separate frying pan, melt the remaining butter over medium-high heat. Then add the beef and brown evenly on all sides. Add the onion, reduce the heat to medium, and cook, stirring occasionally, for 10 minutes or until the onions are golden.

Add the beef and onion to the cider sauce and stir well. Stir in the dill and sour cream. Cook over low heat until thoroughly heated. Be careful not to overcook or the cream will curdle. Serve over noodles or rice.

Cabbage Rolls

Makes 8 large rolls

2 tablespoons oil
1 garlic clove, crushed
1½ teaspoons salt
1½ pounds chuck steak, cut into 1-inch cubes
1 cup dry hard cider
2 cups beef bouillon
3½ cups canned tomatoes, with their juice
1 large onion, coarsely chopped
2 bay leaves
⅛ teaspoon dried rosemary
⅛ teaspoon dried marjoram
¼ teaspoon dried oregano
¼ teaspoon Tabasco Sauce
1 teaspoon freshly ground black pepper
2½ cups cooked rice
1 large head green cabbage

Pour the oil into a large frying pan and heat over high heat. Add the garlic and salt and sauté briefly. Then reduce the heat to medium and add the meat, browning lightly on all sides. Put the meat in a large Dutch oven. Pour in the cider and bouillon and then add the tomatoes, onion and seasonings. Bring the mixture to a boil over high heat, then reduce the heat to medium and cook for 35 minutes or until the meat is tender.

Discard the tough outer leaves from the cabbage and remove the core with a sharp knife. Fill a small Dutch oven three-quarters full with water and bring to a boil over high heat. Place the cabbage in the water with the cut side up. Gently separate the leaves with two large spoons as the outer leaves soften slightly. Remove 8 large leaves and let them drain in a colander.

Remove the meat from the tomato mixture and chop fine. Add the rice to the meat and mix well. Then stir in ¾ cup of the tomato mixture. Place about ½ cup of the beef and rice filling in the center of each cabbage leaf. Fold two sides of the leaf toward the center of the filling, overlapping the edges. Then, starting from the rib end, roll the leaf like a jelly roll. If the rib is too thick, shave it down until it is flexible. Repeat until 8 rolls are made.

Place the rolls tightly together in a long baking pan. Reheat the remaining tomato mixture and pour it over the top. Bake at 350 degrees for 45 minutes.

Good Old Burgers

Makes 3 or 4 large burgers

2 tablespoons butter
1 medium onion, finely chopped
3 slices whole wheat bread, cut into small cubes
¼ cup semi-dry cider
½ pound hamburger
¼ pound pork sausage
1 egg
¼ teaspoon salt

Melt the butter in a medium frying pan and sauté the onion over medium-high heat until it becomes transparent. Place the bread in the pan and stir in to moisten. Then pour in the cider, stir well, and remove from the heat.

Place the hamburger, sausage and egg in a bowl and combine. Sprinkle in the salt, stir in the onion mixture, and blend thoroughly. Form thin hamburger patties and broil in the oven for 5 to 8 minutes on each side.

Pot Roast

Serves 4

2 tablespoons butter
2 cloves garlic, crushed
3-pound boned chuck roast
1 tablespoon flour
½ teaspoon ground thyme
1 teaspoon salt
½ teaspoon ground black pepper
1 cup dry hard cider
1 large onion, quartered
½ cup raisins

Melt the butter in a large Dutch oven, add the garlic, and sauté until lightly browned. Mix the flour, thyme, salt and pepper and rub them into the roast. Brown the roast lightly in the butter and garlic.

Add the onion, cider and raisins and bake, covered, for 2 to 3 hours at 325 degrees.

Tomato Beef

Serves 8

2 tablespoons oil
2 pounds beef round steak or pot roast, thinly sliced
3 garlic cloves, minced
1 large onion, thinly sliced
1 cup mushrooms, thinly sliced
1 teaspoon dried oregano
⅔ cup tomato paste
1½ cups dry hard cider
1 cup beef bouillon

Pour the oil into a Dutch oven and place over high **heat**. When the oil is hot, add the beef and coat evenly with oil. Lightly brown the beef on all sides, then remove it from the pot and set aside.

Add the garlic, onions and mushrooms and sauté over medium-high heat until the onion is transparent. Add the oregano, tomato paste, cider and bouillon and stir well. Reduce the heat to medium and simmer for 20 minutes.

Add the beef to the sauce and simmer for 10 more minutes. Serve over buttered noodles or rice.

Ginger Lamb

Serves 4

3 tablespoons butter
4 large lamb shoulder steaks, boned and cut into small cubes
2 medium onions, thinly sliced
12 small mushrooms, thinly sliced
¾ cup fresh sweet cider
2-inch piece fresh ginger, finely grated
1 tablespoon lemon juice
4 sprigs fresh parsley, finely chopped
Salt and pepper

Put the butter into a medium frying pan and melt over high heat. Brown the lamb evenly in the butter and remove from the pan. Add the onions and mushrooms, reduce the heat to medium, and sauté until the onions are transparent. Pour in the cider, add the ginger, lemon juice and parsley and stir well. Return the meat to the pan and simmer for 15 minutes. Add salt and pepper to taste and serve with side dishes of raisins, peanuts, bananas and zucchini for garnish.

Marinated Lamb

Serves 4

1 cup olive oil
⅔ cup dry hard cider
½ teaspoon ground ginger
½ teaspoon ground cumin
¼ teaspoon salt
¼ teaspoon freshly ground black pepper
2 tablespoons chopped scallions
2½ pounds lamb shoulder steaks or shanks, cut into
    1-inch cubes

Pour the oil and cider into a large bowl and stir until thoroughly blended. Then sprinkle in the ginger, cumin, salt, pepper and scallions and stir well. Place the meat in the liquid and stir to coat each piece evenly with oil mixture. Let it stand for 3 hours, stirring from time to time.

Place the lamb in a medium frying pan over medium-high heat and sauté for several minutes or put on skewers alternating with pieces of tomato, green pepper, pineapple, mushrooms and water chestnuts, and broil for shish kebob.

Roast Leg of Lamb with Cider Mint Sauce

Serves 4 to 6

3-to-4-pound leg of lamb
2 medium garlic cloves, cut in half
2 cups dry hard or semi-dry cider
Salt and pepper

SAUCE
1 cup fresh sweet cider

½ cup cider vinegar
1 teaspoon honey
3 tablespoons fresh mint leaves, finely chopped

Rub the leg of lamb on all sides with garlic, then score the fat side with half-inch gashes and insert the garlic cloves. Place the meat in a roasting pan and pour the cider over the top. Sprinkle the meat lightly with salt and pepper. Cover the pan and bake at 350 degrees for 30 minutes per pound or until the meat next to the bone is pink.

Pour the sweet cider and vinegar into a small saucepan and bring to a boil over high heat. Then add the honey, stir well, and simmer over medium heat for 10 minutes. Add the mint, stir, and simmer for 5 more minutes. Serve warm.

Cidered Ham with Hot Mustard Sauce

Serves 12

1 5-pound ham, bone in, fully cooked
Semi-dry cider
1 cup brown sugar
¼ cup cider vinegar
2 teaspoons dry mustard
12 whole cloves

SAUCE
½ cup hot dry mustard
½ cup flour
½ cup cider vinegar
½ cup sugar
⅛ teaspoon cinnamon
⅛ teaspoon ground cloves
⅛ teaspoon ground allspice
1 tablespoon vegetable oil

Place the ham in a stockpot. Cover with liquid of 3 parts cider and 1 part water. Simmer over medium-low heat for 2 hours or until the ham is thoroughly warmed.

Remove the ham from the pot and reserve the liquid. Remove the skin and score the outside fat diagonally in a diamond pattern, cutting about ½-inch deep. Combine the sugar, vinegar and mustard and pour over the ham, filling the cuts completely. Place a clove or two in each diamond. Bake in a roasting pan at 325 degrees for 2 hours, basting with the warming liquid combined with any remaining vinegar mixture.

Combine the mustard and flour in a small bowl. Pour the vinegar, sugar and spices into a small saucepan and bring to a boil over high heat. Reduce the heat to medium low and simmer for 5 minutes.

Stir into the mustard and flour mixture, add the oil, and stir well. This sauce is also good with pork, tongue and corned beef. It can be made in quantity and will keep indefinitely in the refrigerator.

Ham and Chestnut Pie

Serves 6

Double pie crust
1 pound cooked ham, cut into thin strips
3 egg yolks, hardcooked and mashed
6 large stewed prunes, pitted and cut into halves
12 whole chestnuts, boiled and shelled
12 small mushrooms, cut into thin slices
½ cup dry hard cider
2 tablespoons butter
¼ teaspoon salt
Dash nutmeg
3 tablespoons finely chopped fresh parsley

Roll out a single pie crust and place it in a 10-inch pie pan. Combine the ham, eggs and prunes and stir until the egg lightly coats the ham and prunes. Then add the chestnuts and mushrooms and combine until the filling is thoroughly mixed. Place the filling in the crust and pour the cider over the top. Dot with butter and sprinkle with salt, nutmeg and parsley.

Roll out the top pie crust and place it over the filling. Seal the edges carefully and slash the top 2 or 3 times. Bake at 350 for 50 minutes or until the top of the pie is golden brown.

Pork and Ham Balls

Makes 24 1½-inch balls

1¼ cups dry hard cider
3 slices whole wheat bread, broken into small pieces
1 pound fresh lean pork, ground
½ pound cooked ham, finely ground
1 teaspoon Hot Mustard Sauce, page 95
2 tablespoons fresh parsley, finely chopped
2 eggs, lightly beaten
½ teaspoon freshly ground black pepper
2 tablespoons butter
2 tablespoons oil
Flour

Pour ¼ cup of cider over the bread and let soak for 5 minutes. Add the pork and ham and combine thoroughly. Then blend the mustard sauce, parsley, eggs and pepper together, add to the meat and mix well. Form 1½-inch balls with the meat mixture until it is completely used up. Chill for 30 minutes.

Pour the oil and butter into a large frying pan and place over high heat. Put the balls in the pan and brown evenly on all sides. Transfer them to a Dutch oven and pour off all but 2 tablespoons of fat from the frying pan. Pour in the remaining cider, bring it to a boil, and cook for 2 minutes, scraping the sides of the pan to deglaze. Pour the cider over the meatballs, cover the pan, and bake at 375 degrees for 30 minutes.

Remove the balls from the pan and place on a platter in a warm oven. Shake sufficient flour into the remaining liquid to thicken it. Then pour it over the meatballs as gravy and serve at once.

Savory Spare Ribs

Serves 2 to 3

1 cup dry hard cider
¼ cup oil
¼ cup soy sauce
2 large garlic cloves, mashed
¼ teaspoon Tabasco Sauce
Whole dried chilis
2 pounds country-style spare ribs

Combine the cider, oil and soy and stir until thoroughly blended. Add the garlic, Tabasco and whole chilis to taste.

Pour the sauce over the ribs and let them stand for several hours, basting occasionally, until the meat is thoroughly marinated. Bake in a large baking pan at 350 degrees for 1 hour.

Spicy Spare Ribs

Serves 4

4 pounds country-style spare ribs
1 teaspoon salt
1 large onion, thinly sliced

1 lemon, thinly sliced
2 cups dry hard cider
4 tablespoons brown sugar
1 cup catsup
½ teaspoon nutmeg
2 teaspoons dry hot mustard

Place the spareribs in a large baking pan with the meaty side up. Sprinkle the salt over the top and cover with a layer of onions and then a layer of lemon slices. Bake at 450 degrees for 15 minutes.

Combine the cider, sugar, catsup, nutmeg and mustard in a small saucepan and bring to a boil over high heat. Pour the sauce over the ribs and continue baking at 350 degrees for 1 hour, basting frequently. More cider should be added if the sauce becomes too thick for basting.

Ribs and Kraut

Serves 4

4 cups fresh sauerkraut or
2 16-ounce cans of sauerkraut
½ cup uncooked barley
1½ teaspoons salt
3 pounds spare ribs
3 cups fresh sweet cider

Place the sauerkraut in a large bowl and fill the bowl with water. Stir for several minutes and then drain the sauerkraut.

Add the barley and ½ teaspoon of salt to the sauerkraut. Put two-thirds of the sauerkraut mixture in the bottom of a Dutch oven. Add the spareribs and sprinkle the remaining salt over the top. Cover the meat with the remaining sauerkraut and pour 2 cups of cider over the top. Cover the pot and bake at 400 degrees for 2 hours. Then add the remaining cider and bake until the ribs are tender.

Stuffed Pork Chops with Savory Cider Sauce

Serves 6

6 double pork chops
1 teaspoon salt
1 teaspoon freshly ground black pepper
1 tablespoon bacon fat
1 medium onion, finely chopped
½ cup celery, finely chopped
1 large apple, peeled and finely chopped
⅛ teaspoon ground sage
2 cups pumpernickel or other dark bread crumbs
1 egg, well beaten
½ cup dry hard cider

Sprinkle the pork chops evenly with salt and pepper. Melt the bacon fat in a medium frying pan over medium heat and add the onion, celery, apple and sage. Stir well and sauté until the apple and celery are soft. Add the crumbs and stir well, then add the egg. Blend the entire mixture very thoroughly.

Fill the cavity in the center of each chop with stuffing. Return to the frying pan and brown each chop lightly on both sides. Place in a large baking pan, pour the cider evenly over the top, and cover the pan with foil. Bake at 350 degrees for 45 minutes, basting occasionally with pan juices.

Savory Cider Sauce

1 tablespoon butter
1 teaspoon brown sugar
3 scallions, finely chopped
2 cups semi-dry cider
1 small carrot, peeled and finely chopped

3 whole cloves
4 whole peppercorns
1 small bay leaf
⅛ teaspoon ground thyme
Dash salt

Melt the butter in a small saucepan over medium-high heat. Add the sugar and scallions and sauté for 2 minutes. Pour in the cider and bring the mixture to a boil, then reduce the heat to medium low and simmer for 5 minutes. Add the carrot, cloves, peppercorns, bay leaf, thyme and salt and simmer for 15 minutes. Stir in a little flour to thicken if desired.

When the pork chops are baked, remove from the pan and set aside in a warm oven. Pour the cider sauce into the pan and scrape the sides to deglaze. Then pour the sauce over the chops and serve at once.

Smothered Pork

Serves 4

2 tablespoons butter
4 large rib or loin pork chops
1 large onion, peeled and thinly sliced
¾ cup dry hard cider
1½ teaspoons sesame seeds
½ teaspoon dried whole sage leaves, crushed
½ teaspoon salt
½ teaspoon freshly ground black pepper

Melt the butter in a large frying pan over medium-high heat. Place the chops side by side in the bottom of the pan and brown them evenly on both sides. Then place several onion slices on each chop and pour the cider over the top.

Sprinkle the sesame, sage, salt and pepper evenly over the chops and cover the pan. Reduce the heat to medium and cook for 30 minutes, turning several times, or until the meat at the bone is no longer pink. Flour or cornstarch mixed in a small amount of cider or heavy cream can be added to the pan drippings to make a very flavorful gravy.

Devon Pork Pie

Serves 6

Double pie crust
3 pork loin chops, boned and cut into small pieces
1 large onion, peeled and sliced or
2 large leeks, peeled and thinly sliced
2 large carrots, peeled and thinly sliced
3 medium apples, peeled, cored and thinly sliced
Dash nutmeg
½ teaspoon salt
¼ teaspoon freshly ground black pepper
1 cup dry hard cider
1 tablespoon flour

Place half of the pork in the bottom of a 9-inch pie pan lined with a single pie crust. Cover the pork with a layer of onion or leeks, a layer of carrots, and a layer of apples. Sprinkle the nutmeg over the top along with ¼ teaspoon salt and ⅛ teaspoon pepper.

Repeat the layers with the remaining pork and vegetables and then pour the cider over the top. Sprinkle the remaining salt, pepper and flour evenly over the entire surface.

Roll out the pastry for the top crust and place it on top of the pie. Carefully seal the edges and prick the top in several places with a fork.

Bake at 375 degrees for 15 minutes. Then reduce the temperature to 300 and bake for an additional 40 minutes or until crust is golden.

Roast Pork with Apple Prune Stuffing

Serves 6 to 8

14 dried prunes, pitted
¾ cup dry hard cider
1 tart apple, cored and coarsely chopped
1 medium onion, coarsely chopped
1¼ teaspoons ground thyme
1 teaspoon salt
1 teaspoon pepper
3½-pound pork roast, boned
1 tablespoon flour
½ cup heavy cream

Put the prunes in a small saucepan and pour in the cider. Bring the mixture to a boil over high heat and then at once, setting aside for 30 minutes. Remove the prunes from the liquid, chop coarsely, and place in a bowl. Reserve the liquid. Add the apple, onion, ¼ teaspoon thyme, ¼ teaspoon salt and ¼ teaspoon pepper and combine thoroughly.

Cut a deep pocket in the roast and fill with the prune mixture. Close the opening and tie the roast carefully for baking. Mix the remaining thyme, salt, pepper and flour and rub firmly into the surface. Place the roast in a Dutch oven and pour the reserved liquid into the pan. Cover and cook at 350 degrees for 1½ hours. Remove the cover and cook for 30 more minutes, basting occasionally. When the roast is done, remove it from the pan and add cream to the pan juices.

Traditional Pork and Beans

Serves 8

2½ cups large Northern white beans
1 tablespoon oil
2 garlic cloves, mashed
1 large onion, coarsely chopped
½-pound salt pork, cut into ½-inch pieces
5 cups semi-dry cider
4 tablespoons dark unsulphured molasses
4 tablespoons catsup
2 tablespoons dry hot mustard
2 tablespoons Worcestershire sauce

Cover the beans in a Dutch oven with water. Bring to a boil over high heat and boil for 10 minutes, then turn off the heat and let stand for 2 hours. Drain the beans.

Pour the oil into a medium frying pan and place over high heat. Add the garlic and sauté briefly, then add the onion and salt pork. Sauté for 10 minutes or until the onion is transparent. Then add the cider, molasses, catsup, mustard and Worcestershire and stir very well.

Bring the cider mixture to a boil and pour it over the beans. Stir well and cover the pan. Bake at 325 degrees for 7 hours. Remove the cover and bake for 2 more hours or until the liquid is completely reduced.

Apples Stuffed with Sausage

Serves 4

¾ pound ground pork sausage
1 teaspoon ground allspice
1 teaspoon fresh ginger, finely grated
¼ cup raisins
½ cup dry hard cider
4 large baking apples

Lightly brown the sausage in a medium frying pan over medium heat. Add the allspice and ginger and stir well, then add the raisins and ¼ cup of cider. Reduce the heat to low, cover the pan and simmer until all of the liquid is absorbed and the raisins are plump.

Remove the stem and core from each apple but do not puncture the bottom. Fill the cavity with several tablespoons of the sausage mixture. Then pour the rest of the cider over the top. Bake at 375 degrees for 30 minutes or until the apples are soft.

Glazed Apples and Sausage

Serves 4

1 pound small pork sausages
2 cups fresh sweet cider
4 medium firmly-fleshed apples
⅛ teaspoon salt

Place the sausages in a medium frying pan, pour in the cider and simmer over medium heat for 15 minutes or until the sausages are cooked. Remove the sausages from the pan and bring the liquid to a boil over high heat. When the liquid is reduced to about 1 cup in volume, pour half of it into another pan. Return the sausages to the original pan and simmer over medium heat until they are browned on all sides.

Core the apples, cut into thin slices and sauté in the second pan for several minutes over medium-low heat until they are tender. Sprinkle the salt over the apples, combine them with the sausages, and pour the remaining glaze over the top and serve.

Tomato Sausage Pot

Serves 8

6 tablespoons butter
2 garlic cloves, mashed
1½ cups uncooked rice
2 medium onions, thinly sliced
1 green pepper, coarsely chopped
1½ cups semi-dry cider
2 cups chicken stock
3½ cups canned tomatoes with juice, coarsely chopped
½ pound spicy pork sausage, thinly sliced
¼ teaspoon Tabasco Sauce
1½ teaspoons salt
1 teaspoon freshly ground black pepper
1½ cups grated Cheddar cheese

Melt the butter over high heat in a Dutch oven. Add the garlic and
sauté briefly. Then add the rice and sauté, stirring well, until lightly
browned. Add the onions and green peppers and sauté until the onions are golden. Pour in the cider and stock and stir well. Then add the
tomatoes, sausage, Tabasco, salt and pepper. Blend in the cheese and
cover the pan. Bake at 350 degrees for 35 minutes.

Sautéed Sweetbreads

Serves 4

1 pound beef sweetbreads
½ teaspoon salt
6 tablespoons butter
½ cup dry hard cider

½ cup chicken stock
Flour
½ cup heavy cream
5 large mushrooms, thinly sliced

To prepare the sweetbreads for cooking, soak them in cold salted water for 1 hour. Rinse well and set aside. Bring 2 quarts of water to a boil over high heat and add 4 tablespoons of vinegar and 2 teaspoons of salt. Add the sweetbreads and boil gently for 15 minutes. Drain and cool immediately in cold water. Trim away the tough membranes and tubes.

Cut the sweetbreads into very thin slices. Sprinkle with salt. Melt 4 tablespoons of butter in a medium frying pan over high heat. Sauté the sweetbreads for several minutes until brown on both sides. Remove from the pan and set in a warm oven. Pour the cider and stock into the pan. Simmer over medium heat for 15 minutes or until the liquid reduces by half. Shake sufficient flour over the liquid to thicken it and then pour in the cream, stirring the sauce until it is smooth.

Sauté the mushrooms in the remaining butter until lightly browned. Add them to the sauce and pour the sauce over the sweetbreads. Serve over buttered noodles or rice.

Tongue in Aspic

Serves 4 to 6

1 beef tongue
2 cups dry hard cider
Water
1 onion, coarsely chopped
8 whole peppercorns
15 whole juniper berries, crushed
2 large bay leaves

4 cloves
4 whole allspice
¼ teaspoon Tabasco Sauce
1 tablespoon salt
2 envelopes powdered gelatin
2 tablespoons plus 1 teaspoon lemon juice
3 egg whites

Place the tongue in a large saucepan. Pour in the cider and fill with water to cover the tongue. Add the onion and seasonings and bring to a boil over high heat. Reduce the heat to medium low, cover the pan, and simmer for 3 hours.

Remove the tongue from the pan and chill the stock. Remove the fat that forms on the top. Use 5 cups of clarified stock for the aspic; if there is not enough in the pan, add beef bouillon. To clarify the stock, strain the liquid and bring it to a boil over high heat. Beat the egg whites until stiff and add them to the hot stock, stirring rapidly for one minute. Remove the mixture from the heat and strain through a clean dishcloth or other tightly-woven cloth.

Measure 4 cups of heated stock and set aside. In a separate bowl, pour in ¾ cup stock and add the gelatin. Stir until the gelatin dissolves, then add the lemon juice and stir well. Combine the gelatin mixture with the rest of the stock and stir well.

Slice the tongue very thin and lay the slices in a loaf pan. Pour the gelatin mixture over the top and chill until firmly set. Serve with Hot Mustard Sauce, page 95.

Tripe à la Mode de Caen

Serves 12

1 large carrot, peeled and thinly sliced
1 large stalk celery, thinly sliced
4 leeks, peeled and thinly sliced
3 medium onions, thinly sliced
3 pounds cleaned tripe, cut into ½-by-3-inch strips
4 pig's trotters
2 garlic cloves, mashed
1 bay leaf
½ teaspoon crushed thyme
2 teaspoons salt
½ teaspoon black pepper
Dash Tabasco Sauce
1 small onion, stuck with 2 cloves
Dry hard cider to cover
½ cup Calvados
Vinegar

Arrange the carrot, celery, leeks and onions in the bottom of a large Dutch oven. Don't use cast iron as it will darken the tripe. Add the tripe and trotters, then the garlic, bay leaf, thyme, salt, Tabasco and pepper.

Bury the cloved onion and pour in enough cider to cover the rest of the ingredients. Add the Calvados and cover the pot very tightly, using a dampened and floured cloth at the seam between the pot and its cover to prevent any evaporation of liquid.

Bake 7 to 10 hours at 300 degrees or until the tripe is softened. Let the pot cool, then add vinegar to taste. Let the pot stand overnight, remove the trotters, and reheat for serving.

The preparation time of this recipe can be shortened substantially by cooking the tripe and trotters in a stainless steel pressure cooker at 15 pounds pressure with the spices and some of the vegetables for 50 minutes. Then add the remaining vegetables and cook another 10 minutes.

Jellies, Condiments and Preserves

Although cider loses much of its apple flavor when exposed to heat, sweet or dry cider can be used very successfully in Cider Mint Jelly, and as a fruit additive to Cider Strawberry Jelly. Sweet cider is often used commercially to stretch the amount of fruit in jellies and preserves, not only because of its natural sweetness but because it contains a lot of pectin.

Cider is also a valuable addition to the canning process of preserving fruit. Its substantial sugar content means that when water is replaced with cider in canning, less additional sugar is needed. When fresh cider is used to can an exceptionally sweet fruit like sweet cherries, no additional sugar is generally required. Since both batches of fruit and jugs of cider vary in natural sweetness, a small amount should be combined and tested before a decision about more sugar is made. Those diet and health conscious cooks who have reduced or eliminated sugar from most of their food will be especially pleased with the results of canning with cider.

In addition to sweet cherries, ripe plums, pears, raspberries and even pie cherries lend themselves well to canning in fresh sweet cider. Peaches and apricots do not, however, probably because their flavors are simply too delicate.

Jars filled with canned fruit and cider can be processed by a traditional method such as the boiling water bath for 25 minutes, or fruit can be cooked in cider for 20 minutes and then put into jars. Both methods require careful sealing of the lids and very clean equipment.

Dry cider is an improvement in many traditional pickling recipes which specify water, vinegar and sugar. As when canning fruit, the cook should test the recipe in small quantities to determine the proper amount of cider before working with all of the vegetables at hand.

Apple Butter

Makes 3 pints

1 cup fresh sweet cider or cider concentrate
8 cups apples, peeled, cored and coarsely chopped
2½ cups sugar or ⅓ to ½ cup sugar for each cup of
*   cooked pulp*
1 cinnamon stick, broken into bits
1 whole clove
1 whole allspice

Place the cider and apples in a large saucepan and bring to a boil over high heat. Reduce the heat to medium low and simmer for 20 minutes or until the apples are soft. When the apples are cooked put them through a sieve.

Combine the sugar with the strained apples and blend well. Place the cinnamon, clove and allspice in a small mesh bag and hide it in the center of the apple mixture. Cover the pan and bake at 300 degrees for 1 hour, stirring frequently, until the desired thickness is reached. Remove the spice bag and spoon into jars.

Applesauce

Makes 3 quarts

11 cups apples, peeled, cored and thinly sliced
3 cups fresh sweet cider
1 cup sugar

Place the cider, apples and sugar in a small Dutch oven and bring to a boil over high heat. Reduce the heat to medium low and simmer for 50 minutes or until the apples are soft. Serve chunk-style or put through a food mill.

Cider Mint Jelly

Makes 4 half pints

1¾ cups fresh sweet or dry hard cider
3 cups sugar
½ bottle liquid pectin
4 large fresh mint leaves
1 tablespoon sugar
2 tablespoons cider vinegar

Combine the cider and sugar in the top of a double boiler and bring the water in the boiler to a boil over high heat. Cook the cider and sugar for 5 minutes, stirring constantly, until the sugar dissolves.

Remove the entire pot from the heat and leave intact to keep the jelly over hot water. Stir in the pectin, then skim the foam that forms. Pour jelly into sterilized jars and cool. Wash mint leaves well. Pour the vinegar into a small saucepan, stir in 1 additional tablespoon of sugar, and bring to a boil over high heat. Remove from the heat and drop in the mint leaves. Cover and let stand for several minutes. Lay one mint leaf on top of the jelly in each jar, then seal the jars with paraffin. Jelly may take several days to set.

Cider Strawberry Jelly

Makes 3 half pints

2 tablespoons lemon juice
1 cup fresh sweet cider
1 cup puréed strawberries
3¾ cups sugar
½ bottle liquid pectin

Pour the lemon juice, cider, berries and sugar into a small saucepan. Bring the mixture to a rolling boil over high heat, stirring rapidly. Immediately add the pectin, return to a boil, and cook for one minute, stirring constantly.

Remove from the heat, skim the foam that forms, and pour into clean jars, leaving ½-inch of head room at the top. Seal with paraffin.

Cranberry Walnut Sauce

Makes about 5 cups

1 cup fresh sweet cider
½ cup sugar
4 cups whole cranberries
2 teaspoons grated orange peel
1 cup walnuts, finely chopped

Combine the cider and sugar in a large saucepan and bring to a boil over high heat. Reduce heat and cook for 5 minutes, stirring constantly. Add the cranberries, orange peel and walnuts and stir, returning the sauce to a boil. Reduce the heat to medium low and simmer for 15 minutes or until the cranberries begin to burst. Keep refrigerated.

Fruit Compote

Serves 6

1 cup fresh pineapple, cut into small chunks
2 cups fresh peaches, thinly sliced
1 cup fresh strawberries, each cut in half
¾ cup applesauce
4 teaspoons lemon peel, finely grated
½ cup fresh sweet cider

1½ teaspoons ground cinnamon
1 teaspoon ground nutmeg
½ teaspoon ground ginger

Combine the pineapple, peaches and strawberries with the apple-sauce, lemon peel and cider. Put the fruit mixture into a square baking pan and sprinkle the cinnamon, nutmeg and ginger evenly over the top. Bake at 250 degrees for 40 minutes.

Prune Chestnut Sauce

Makes about 2 cups

¾ cup dry hard cider
¼ teaspoon ground ginger
1 tablespoon butter
12 fresh chestnuts, boiled and shelled
8 large pitted, stewed prunes

Pour the cider into a small saucepan and stir in the ginger. Bring the liquid to a boil over high heat and then add the butter. Reduce the heat to medium low as soon as the butter melts and add the chestnuts and prunes. Simmer for 10 minutes. Serve warm with ham or fowl.

This sauce improves in flavor with age and should be made in larger quantity for use over several months. Keep refrigerated.

Spiced Plums

¾ cup semi-dry cider
½ cinnamon stick
3 whole cloves
3 whole allspice, broken
8 large fresh pitted plums
½ lemon, cut into 3 or 4 thin slices

Bring the cider to a boil over high heat in a small saucepan. Then add the cinnamon, cloves and allspice. Reduce the heat to medium low and simmer for 5 minutes. Add the plums and lemon slices, stir well, and cover the pan. Simmer for 15 minutes or until the plums are soft. Serve with pork or game.

Vegetables and Side Dishes

Sweet and semi-dry cider enhances the natural sweetness of vegetables. Candied Yams, Beets in Cider Orange Sauce and Cinnamon Squash are all made more flavorful with the addition of cider as the cooking liquid. Almost any vegetable — from leeks to rutabagas — will taste better steamed or sautéed if a little cider is added to the liquid.

Dry cider adds zest to Leeks Braised in Cider and Ratatouille that would also be provided by dry white wine. Savory Rice makes such a delicious accompaniment to almost any meat or fowl dish that plain steamed rice will probably never be served in our kitchens again.

Beets in Cider Orange Sauce

Serves 3 to 4

2 tablespoons butter
2 tablespoons flour
½ cup fresh orange juice
½ cup fresh sweet cider
2½ cups cooked beets, thinly sliced
Salt

Melt the butter in a medium saucepan over high heat and stir in the flour. Reduce the heat to medium low and cook the mixture for two minutes, stirring constantly. Then pour in the orange juice and cider and stir until smooth. Simmer for 10 minutes, stirring occasionally.

Add the beets and a pinch of salt and stir well. Simmer for 5 minutes and serve warm.

Pickled Beets

Makes 3 pints

1¾ *cups cider vinegar*
¾ *cup fresh sweet cider*
¾ *cup sugar*
½ *teaspoon salt*
6 whole allspice
½ *cinnamon stick, broken into small pieces*
15 medium beets, peeled, cooked and thinly sliced

Pour the vinegar and cider into a large saucepan and bring to a boil over high heat. Reduce the heat to medium low, stir in the sugar, salt, allspice and cinnamon and simmer for 15 minutes. Strain the liquid, return to the saucepan, and bring it to a boil. Strain the liquid again.

Divide the beets evenly into canning jars. Pour liquid into each jar to cover the beets and leave ½-inch of head room. Seal by your favorite method or chill and serve at once.

Puget Sound Baked Beans

Serves 8 to 12

2 pounds dried black-eyed beans
5 cups water
4 cups dry hard cider

1 pound salt pork, diced
2 medium onions, cut into quarters
3½ cups canned tomatoes, with juice
¼ teaspoon dried oregano
¼ teaspoon dried rosemary
¼ teaspoon dried basil
¼ teaspoon dried marjoram
3 large garlic cloves, mashed
¼ teaspoon pepper
¼ teaspoon salt

Wash and drain the beans. Pour the water into a large Dutch oven, add the beans and bring to a boil over high heat for 5 minutes. Remove from the heat and let stand for 1 hour.

Pour in the cider and add the pork, onions, tomatoes, herbs and pepper. Stir well, bring to a boil over high heat, and cook for 5 minutes. Bake, covered, at 300 degrees for 6 hours. Add salt to taste before serving.

Green Beans, Ham and Cheese

Serves 4

2 cups mature green beans, cut into ½-inch pieces
1 cup cooked ham, cubed
⅔ cup fresh sweet cider
Swiss cheese

Put the beans, ham and cider in a square baking dish and cover. Bake at 350 degrees for 20 minutes or until the beans are tender. Remove from the oven and place several slices of cheese on top. Return to the oven and bake uncovered for 5 minutes or until the cheese completely melts.

Carrots Glazed with Cider

Serves 4

2 tablespoons butter
¼ cup fresh sweet cider
1 sprig fresh mint
2 cups diced carrots

Put the butter, cider and one mint leaf into a small saucepan and bring to a boil over high heat. Reduce the heat to medium low, add the carrots and simmer for 10 minutes until the carrots are tender but not too soft. Remove the cooked mint leaf and garnish with more fresh mint.

Leeks Braised in Cider

Serves 4

6 large leeks, washed and trimmed
½ teaspoon salt
¼ teaspoon freshly ground black pepper
3 slices slab bacon, diced
1½ cups dry hard cider

Place the leeks in the bottom of a small Dutch oven. Sprinkle the salt and pepper over the top and add the bacon. Pour in the cider and bake, covered, at 350 degrees for 1 hour or until the leeks are tender and the liquid is greatly reduced.

Ratatouille

Serves 8

4 tablespoons olive oil
2 medium sweet onions, peeled and thinly sliced
2 garlic cloves, mashed
½ cup pitted black olives, cut into halves
2 cups diced eggplant
3 green peppers, cut into 1-inch pieces
2 stalks celery, thinly sliced
1 medium carrot, peeled and thinly sliced
1 medium zucchini, thinly sliced
3 large tomatoes, cut into bite-size chunks
½ cup dry hard cider
½ teaspoon salt

Pour the oil into a large frying pan and place over high heat. Add the onions and sauté until golden. Then add the garlic, olives and vegetables. Pour the cider over top, sprinkle in the salt and stir the mixture well. Cover and simmer over low heat for 45 minutes. Remove the lid and cook for 10 more minutes or until liquid is greatly reduced.

Risotto

Serves 6

4 slices slab bacon, diced
1 medium onion, diced
2 garlic cloves, mashed
1 cup uncooked white rice
Dash cayenne pepper
½ medium green pepper, cut into julienne strips
¼ medium sweet red pepper or several pimientos,
    cut into julienne strips

10 pitted black olives, cut into halves
1 cup dry hard cider
1 cup water
½ pound fresh Parmesan or Cheddar cheese, grated

Fry the bacon in a large frying pan over medium heat until it is almost crisp. Then add the onion and garlic and sauté until transparent. Add the rice and stir constantly, cooking until it becomes lightly browned. Then add the cayenne, peppers, olives, cider and water and cover with a tight lid. Reduce the heat to low and cook for 20 minutes or until all of the cooking liquid is absorbed and the rice is thoroughly cooked.

Sprinkle the cheese over the top and place the pan under the oven broiler for several minutes or until the cheese melts. Serve at once.

Savory Rice

Serves 4

1½ cups water
½ cup semi-dry or dry hard cider
2 cubes chicken bouillon
1 cup uncooked white rice

Bring the water and cider to a boil over high heat in a medium saucepan. Add the bouillon and stir until the cubes are completely dissolved. Pour in the rice, stir once and cover. Reduce the heat to low and simmer for 20 minutes or until the liquid is completely absorbed and the rice is soft.

Cinnamon Squash

Serves 4

2 acorn squash or other firm-fleshed winter variety
2 tablespoons butter
½ teaspoon ground cinnamon
1 cup fresh sweet cider

Cut the acorn squash in half, clean, and place shell-side down in a long baking pan. Dot with butter, sprinkle with cinnamon and pour the cider into the bottom of the pan. Put foil over the top of the pan and seal the edges.

Bake at 350 degrees for 30 minutes or until the squash is very tender.

Candied Yams

Serves 4

3 tablespoons butter
2 tablespoons brown sugar
2 large yams, scored lengthwise in several places
1½ cups fresh sweet cider
½ teaspoon freshly ground nutmeg
2 tablespoons fresh lemon peel, coarsely grated
2 tablespoons fresh orange peel, coarsely grated

Cream the butter and sugar together until thoroughly blended. Place the yams in a large baking pan and rub the butter mixture evenly over the skin and into the cuts. Then pour the cider over top and sprinkle evenly with nutmeg and citrus peel.

Bake at 350 degrees for 50 minutes or until the yams are tender when pierced with a fork.

Although almost all of the following dessert recipes call for fresh sweet cider, semi-dry cider can often be substituted, especially if a little less sweetness is desired. Cooking must be very limited or concentrated cider should be used if much apple flavor is desired. Cooking can also caramelize the natural sugars in cider, so care must be taken when it is exposed to heat.

Cider Meringue Pie

Makes one 9-inch pie

2 cups concentrated sweet cider
½ cup sugar
Pinch salt
5 tablespoons cornstarch
3 egg yolks, lightly beaten
3 tablespoons butter

MERINGUE
3 egg whites
1½ tablespoons sugar
1 tablespoon concentrated sweet cider
Pinch salt
Baked 9-inch pie shell

Pour 1½ cups of cider into the top of a double boiler, stir in the sugar and salt, and bring to a gentle boil over high heat. Dissolve the cornstarch in the remaining cider and add to the hot cider, stirring constantly until the mixture thickens and clears.

Add the egg yolks to the cider mix, stirring rapidly. Cover the pan and cook the filling for 10 minutes, stirring occasionally. Remove from the heat and stir in the butter. Cool and pour into a baked pie shell.

Beat the egg whites until very stiff, adding the sugar, cider and salt. Spread the meringue evenly over the pie and bake at 300 degrees for 15 minutes or until the meringue is golden.

Cider Walnut Pie

Makes one 9-inch pie

2 cups fresh sweet cider
1 cup dark brown sugar
4 tablespoons butter, melted
4 eggs, well beaten
2 teaspoons lemon juice
½ cup walnuts, finely ground
Baked 9-inch pie shell
Whipping cream

Pour the cider into a medium saucepan and bring to a boil over high heat. Then add the sugar, reduce the heat to medium, and cook for 10 minutes, stirring continually, until the sugar dissolves and the mixture becomes slightly syrupy. Pour in the melted butter and stir well. Remove from the heat and let the mixture cool.

Beat the eggs until frothy and then pour in the cooled cider mixture, stirring well. Add the lemon juice and stir, then add the walnuts. Pour the entire mixture into the baked pie shell and bake at 375 degrees for 30 minutes or until center of the pie is firm. Serve either warm or at room temperature with whipping cream on top.

Golden Carrot Pie

2 eggs
½ cup sugar
Dash ground nutmeg
¼ teaspoon ground cinnamon
⅛ teaspoon ground ginger
Pinch salt
1 cup cooked carrots, riced or mashed
½ cup fresh sweet cider
½ cup heavy cream
9-inch pie shell

Beat the eggs, sugar, nutmeg, cinnamon, ginger and salt until thoroughly blended. Add the carrots and stir well. Then pour in the cider and cream and stir until completely blended.

Pour the filling into the pie shell and bake at 350 degrees for 35 minutes or until a knife inserted in the center comes clean. Serve with whipped cream.

Mincemeat Pie

Makes 3 10-inch pies

1 pound beefsteak or roast, cut into 1-inch cubes
Semi-dry cider
1 cup ground suet
2 cups mixed candied fruit
1 cup currants
1 cup golden raisins
Grated rind of 1 lemon
¼ cup fresh lemon juice
2 cups dry hard cider

2 cups blackberry juice
1 teaspoon ground cinnamon
1 teaspoon ground cloves
1 teaspoon ground nutmeg
1 teaspoon ground mace
1 teaspoon salt
1 teaspoon finely ground black pepper
3 cups brown sugar
5 cups diced, peeled, tart apples
1 cup Calvados
3 10-inch pie shells with top crusts

Cook the beef until tender over medium heat in a covered small frying pan with enough semi-dry cider to cover. Cool and put it through a grinder or processor. Put the ground meat in a large bowl and stir in the suet, candied fruit, currants, raisins, lemon rind and juice, cider and berry juice. Stir the mixture well and sprinkle in the spices, salt and pepper. Stir until thoroughly combined and add the brown sugar and apples. Stir once again and let the mixture stand overnight to absorb flavor.

Place in a Dutch oven and bake at 300 degrees for 1 to 2 hours or until the apples are tender, stirring occasionally. Pour in the Calvados and stir well. Fill the pie shells and bake at 450 degrees for 10 minutes, then reduce to 350 degrees and bake for 30 minutes.

Pumpkin Pie

Makes one 9-inch pie

2 large eggs, lightly beaten
2 cups cooked fresh pumpkin or
1 16-ounce can pumpkin
3 tablespoons cornstarch
1 cup sugar

½ teaspoon ground cinnamon
⅛ teaspoon ground ginger
⅛ teaspoon ground cloves
1⅓ tablespoons melted butter
½ cup heavy cream
1 cup fresh sweet cider
9-inch pie shell

Combine the eggs and pumpkin and stir until thoroughly blended. In a separate bowl, combine the cornstarch, sugar, cinnamon, ginger and cloves and stir until well blended. Add the dry ingredients to the pumpkin mixture and blend thoroughly. Then pour in the butter, cream and cider and stir well.

Pour the pumpkin mixture into the pie shell and bake at 400 degrees for 15 minutes. Reduce the heat to 350 degrees and bake 30 minutes more.

Butter Rum Cider Cake

Serves 12

3 cups sifted flour
2 teaspoons baking soda
1 teaspoon salt
½ teaspoon ground allspice
½ teaspoon ground nutmeg
½ teaspoon ground cinnamon
¾ cup butter, at room temperature
1½ cups firmly packed brown sugar
3 eggs
1 cup fresh sweet cider
¾ cup milk
Apricot jam

Grease three 8-inch round cake pans and line with greased wax paper. Preheat the oven to 350 degrees.

Sift the flour, baking soda, salt and spices together and set aside. Cream the butter and sugar until thoroughly blended. Beat the eggs one at a time into the butter mixture. In another small bowl, pour the cider and milk together and stir well.

Add the flour mixture and liquid alternately to the creamed mixture, beating well after each addition. Pour the batter into the pans and bake for 25 minutes or until a cake tester comes clean when it is inserted in the center. Place the pans on wire racks to cool. After 10 minutes, remove each layer from its pan. Spread apricot jam between the layers and frost with Butter Rum Frosting.

BUTTER RUM FROSTING
½ cup soft butter
1 teaspoon rum extract
1½ cups powdered sugar
¼ cup honey

Cream the butter and extract until thoroughly blended. Add the sugar gradually to the butter, stirring well, alternating with additions of honey. If the frosting is not sufficiently stiff, add a little more sugar.

This amount of frosting will cover the cake but won't fill between the layers.

Chocolate Applesauce Cake

Makes 9 3-inch squares

2 cups flour
1 cup sugar
2 teaspoons soda
1 teaspoon ground cinnamon
½ teaspoon ground nutmeg

2 tablespoons cocoa
1 tablespoon cornstarch
1 egg, beaten
1 teaspoon vanilla extract
1½ cups hot applesauce
½ cup melted butter
½ cup fresh sweet cider

Combine the flour, sugar, soda, cinnamon, nutmeg, cocoa and corn-starch and stir until thoroughly blended. Pour in the egg, vanilla, applesauce, melted butter and cider and stir.

Bake in a greased and floured long baking pan at 350 degrees for 40 minutes.

Cardamom Cake

Makes 9 3-inch squares

1 cup butter, at room temperature
2 cups sugar
3 eggs, lightly beaten
¾ cup fresh sweet cider
½ teaspoon vanilla extract
4 cups flour
1 teaspoon baking soda
1½ teaspoons ground cardamom

Cream the butter and sugar together until thoroughly blended. Then add the eggs and beat well. Pour in the cider and vanilla and stir until the mixture is smooth.

Combine the flour, baking soda and cardamon until well blended. Add the dry ingredients to the butter and egg mixture and stir until batter is smooth. Pour the batter into a greased and floured square baking pan and bake at 375 degrees for 50 minutes or until a cake tester comes clean when inserted in the center. Frost with Fluffy Cider Frosting (next page).

FLUFFY CIDER FROSTING

Makes about 1 cup

1 egg white, chilled
1 cup sugar
¼ teaspoon cream of tartar
½ cup concentrated sweet cider

Combine the egg white, sugar and cream of tartar until thoroughly blended. Bring the cider to a boil over high heat in a small saucepan. Pour the hot cider into the egg mixture and beat vigorously. Continue beating for several minutes until the frosting is stiff.

Cider Milk Cake

Serves 12

2 cups sugar
½ cup shortening
2 tablespoons cocoa
1 cup milk
1 cup fresh sweet or semi-dry cider
3 cups flour
2 teaspoons baking soda
1 teaspoon ground cinnamon
½ teaspoon ground cloves
½ teaspoon ground nutmeg
¼ teaspoon salt
½ cup raisins

Cream the sugar, shortening and cocoa until thoroughly blended. Combine the milk and cider. Mix the flour, baking soda, spices and salt together. Add the flour mixture to the liquid, then combine with the sugar mixture and beat until the batter is smooth. Stir in the raisins and bake in a long baking pan at 350 degrees for 40 minutes or until cake tester comes clean when inserted in the center.

Cider Sponge Cake

Serves 12

1½ cups flour
¼ teaspoon baking soda
1½ teaspoons baking powder
½ teaspoon salt
1¼ cup sugar
4 eggs, separated
¼ teaspoon cream of tartar
½ cup fresh sweet cider
4 tablespoons melted butter
1 teaspoon vanilla

Combine the flour, baking soda, baking powder, salt and ¾ cup of sugar until thoroughly blended. Beat the egg whites until stiff, slowly adding the cream of tartar and remaining sugar.

Beat the egg yolks until they are creamy. Pour in the cider, butter and vanilla and stir well. Then add the flour mixture a little at a time, stirring after each addition until the batter is well blended.

Fold the batter carefully into the egg whites. Bake in a greased and floured long baking pan at 325 degrees for 25 minutes or until the center springs back when touched with a fork. If the top of the cake is browning too quickly, cover the pan loosely with aluminum foil for the last 10 minutes of baking. Let the cake cool in the pan.

Serve with several spoonfuls of cider over the top and whipped cream, or layered with cider filling from Cider Meringue Pie, page 123, and topped with whipped cream.

Cottage Pudding

1½ cups flour
2 teaspoons baking powder
3 tablespoons sugar
3 egg yolks, beaten
4 tablespoons melted butter
½ cup light cream
¼ cup fresh sweet cider
½ teaspoon vanilla extract

SAUCE
4 cups sweet cider
8 tablespoons sugar
4 tablespoons cornstarch

Sift the flour, baking powder and sugar together. Combine the egg yolks, butter, cream, cider and vanilla and stir until thoroughly blended. Add the dry ingredients to the egg mixture and stir until batter is smooth. Pour 3¾ cups of cider and the sugar into a small saucepan and bring to a boil over high heat, stirring constantly. Dissolve the cornstarch in the remaining cider and add to the cider in the pan, stirring rapidly until the mixture thickens and clears. Remove from the heat immediately and pour into a square baking pan. Spoon the batter into the sauce in the pan and bake at 450 degrees for 20 minutes.

Sour Cream Spice Cake

Serves 12

1 cup sugar
½ cup sour cream
3 eggs

1 cup fresh sweet cider
¼ cup oil
4 cups flour
2 teaspoons baking soda
½ teaspoon ground allspice
½ teaspoon ground cloves
1 teaspoon ground ginger or
½ teaspoon ground ginger and
½ teaspoon grated fresh ginger

Combine the sugar and sour cream until thoroughly blended. Add the eggs one at a time and beat well. Pour in the cider and oil and stir until the mixture is smooth. Combine the flour with the baking soda, allspice, cloves and ginger. Add the dry mixture gradually to the sour cream mixture, stirring well after each addition. When the batter is smooth, stir in the fresh ginger.

Bake at 350 degrees in a greased and floured long baking pan for 50 minutes or until a cake tester inserted in the center comes out clean. Serve with whipped cream.

Fluffy Oven-Baked Doughnuts

1½ to 2 dozen doughnuts and
2 dozen doughnut holes

1 medium potato, peeled, cooked and mashed
¼ cup warm potato water
2 packages (2 tablespoons) active dry yeast
1½ cups semi-dry cider, warmed in the top of a
*   double boiler over hot water*
1 cup dry milk solids
½ cup sugar
1 teaspoon salt
1 teaspoon ground nutmeg

¼ teaspoon ground cinnamon
2 eggs, at room temperature
½ cup shortening
4½ cups all-purpose flour
½ cup melted butter, divided into two portions

CINNAMON SUGAR
½ cup sugar
1 teaspoon cinnamon

Dissolve the yeast in the warm potato water. Add the potato and set the mixture aside until it is bubbly. Then beat in the cider, milk solids, sugar, salt, nutmeg, cinnamon, eggs and shortening using an electric beater on medium speed.

Add 4 cups of flour, one cup at a time, beating after each addition. Turn beater to high speed when dough becomes stiff. Stir in the remaining flour with a spoon. The dough will be very sticky. Cover and let it rise in a warm place for 1 hour.

Put flour on your hands and shift the dough from the bowl to an evenly floured board. Do not knead. Sprinkle the top evenly with flour. Roll gently with a floured rolling pin to ½ inch, making sure that the dough remains in contact with the floured surface.

Cut out the doughnuts with a 2-inch doughnut cutter.

Cut as many from the rolled dough as possible. Do not reroll the excess, as the additional flour has changed the dough so that it will not bake properly.

Carefully place each doughnut and doughnut hole 2 inches apart on greased baking sheets. Brush them generously with half the melted butter and let rise until doubled, usually about 20 to 30 minutes.

Preheat the oven to 450 degrees and place the oven racks in the top half of the oven. When the doughnuts are ready to bake, reduce the heat to 400 degrees and put them in for 8 to 10 minutes. Remove from the oven and brush with the remaining melted butter, then roll the doughnuts in the cinnamon sugar. Cool on a rack and cover with a clean cloth. Return the oven to 450 degrees before baking the remaining doughnuts.

Oatmeal Cookies

Makes 24 3-inch cookies

½ cup butter, at room temperature
½ cup firmly packed brown sugar
½ cup sugar
1 egg
½ cup concentrated sweet cider
1 cup flour
½ teaspoon baking soda
½ teaspoon baking powder
½ teaspoon salt
1 cup uncooked quick rolled oats

Cream the butter and sugars together until thoroughly blended. Beat the egg and cider together until smooth, pour into the butter mixture, and beat again until smooth.

Combine the flour, baking soda, baking powder and salt in a separate bowl and gradually add them to the butter mixture. Stir in the oats and beat until thoroughly blended.

Bake at 350 degrees on a well-greased baking sheet for 10 minutes or until the cookies turn light brown.

Apple Cream

Serves 4

1 cup fresh sweet cider
½ cup light brown sugar
2-inch piece fresh ginger, peeled and finely grated
Dash ground nutmeg
4 medium apples, peeled, cored and cut into thick slices
1 cup heavy cream

Pour the cider and sugar into a medium saucepan and bring it to a boil over high heat, stirring until the sugar dissolves. Reduce the heat to medium low and simmer for 5 minutes. Then add the ginger and nutmeg and stir well.

Place the apples in the liquid and simmer over low heat for 15 minutes or until the apples are soft. Set the cooked apples aside to cool. When the apples are warm but not hot, pour in the cream and stir well. Serve at once.

Baked Apples with Ciderschaum

Serves 4

4 large baking apples, cored and peeled ⅔ of the
    way to the base
Peel from ½ large orange
1 cup fresh sweet cider
1 cup water
1 inch vanilla bean

SAUCE
1 cup semi-dry cider
¼ cup water
2 whole eggs
½ cup sugar

Place the apple peelings and cores in the bottom of a large baking pan and add the orange peel, cider, water and vanilla bean. Place a wire rack over the top of the pan and place the apples on the rack. Cover and steam the apples in a 350 degree oven for 20 minutes or until the fruit is tender.

Remove the pan from the heat and spoon the liquid over the apples until they become cool.

Combine the cider, water, eggs and sugar in the top of a double boiler and cook over hot but not boiling water. Beat the mixture with a whisk for 20 minutes or until the foam subsides and the sauce is slightly thickened. Serve either warm or cold by spooning over the apples. Garnish with glacéed cherries.

Baked Apples with Raisin Sauce

Serves 4

4 medium apples, cored and hollowed in center
1 cup raisins
2 cups fresh sweet cider
½ cup sugar
½ cup water
¼ lemon, unpeeled, cut into chunks
1 tablespoon cornstarch

Place the apples in a large baking pan. Soak the raisins in ¾ cup of cider and water until they are plump. Put the raisins and liquid in a medium saucepan, add the sugar and lemon and bring the mixture to a boil over high heat, stirring well. Reduce the heat to medium low and simmer for 10 minutes, stirring occasionally. Dissolve the cornstarch in ¼ cup of cider and add to the hot cider. Simmer, stirring, until the mixture thickens and clears.

Fill each apple cavity with two spoons of raisin sauce. Pour the remaining cider over the top to fill the pan with 1 inch of liquid. Cover and bake at 300 degrees for 30 minutes or until the apples are tender.

Blushing Apples

6 medium firmly-fleshed apples, cored and peeled
⅔ of the way to the base
1 cup frozen raspberries, forced through a sieve
½ cup sugar
1½ cups fresh sweet cider

FILLING
1 tablespoon butter
1 tablespoon sugar
1 teaspoon cornstarch
4 tablespoons walnuts, finely chopped

Place the apples upside-down in a large baking pan. Strain the raspberries. Pour ½ cup of the raspberry juice into a small saucepan and add the cider and sugar. Stir the mixture well and bring to a boil over high heat. Pour the liquid over the apples and bake at 325 degrees for 20 minutes or until the apples are almost soft.

Melt the butter in the top of a double boiler and pour in ½ cup of the raspberry purée. Stir in the cornstarch and sugar and stir until the mixture thickens and clears. Add the walnuts and remove from the heat.

Turn the apples over in the pan and fill the centers with the raspberry mixture. Return to the oven for 10 minutes, or until the apples are softened, basting with liquid from the pan.

Chill and serve with whipped cream.

Poached Pears

4 medium pears, peeled with stems left intact
3 cups water
3 cups fresh sweet cider
12 whole cloves
1 large cinnamon stick, broken into pieces
2 lemon slices
¼ cup Calvados

Pour the water and cider into a large saucepan and bring to a boil over high heat. Stir in the cloves and cinnamon and add the lemon slices. Reduce the heat to medium, cover the pan and simmer for 10 minutes.

Place the pears carefully in the liquid, then pour in the Calvados. Simmer, not allowing the liquid to boil, for 12 minutes or until the pears are soft.

Frozen Cider Delight

Serves 6

2 large oranges
1 large lemon
2 medium bananas
2 cups fresh sweet cider
1 cup sugar

Squeeze the oranges and lemons to extract the juice. Mash the bananas and pour in the juice. Stir well and add the cider and sugar. Pour into a small tray and freeze for 1 hour. Stir several times during freezing to break up the crystals.

Cider Sherbet

Serves 8

1 package (1 tablespoon) unflavored powdered gelatin
1¼ cup cold water
¾ cup sugar
2 cups fresh sweet or semi-dry cider
½ cup fresh lemon juice
1 egg white, beaten until stiff

Dissolve the gelatin in ¼ cup of water. Pour the remaining water into a medium saucepan and bring to a boil over high heat. Stir in the sugar and boil for 2 minutes or until sugar is completely dissolved. Add the gelatin and stir well. Chill this mixture. Then pour in the cider and lemon juice and stir. Fold in the egg white, pour into individual serving dishes and freeze. Stir occasionally during freezing.

Cider Whip

Serves 6

2 cups concentrated sweet cider
½ cup sugar
Pinch salt
5 tablespoons cornstarch
3 eggs, separated
3 tablespoons melted butter
½ cup walnuts, finely chopped

Pour 1½ cups of cider into the top of a double boiler and bring to a boil over high heat. Remove from the heat and stir in the sugar, reserving 1 tablespoon for later use, and add the salt. Dissolve the cornstarch in the remaining cider and add to the hot cider. Beat the liquid with a whisk until it thickens.

Lightly beat the egg yolks and add to the thickened cider, stirring rapidly until well blended. Place the mixture over gently boiling water, cover the pan, and cook for 10 minutes. Remove from the heat, add the butter and stir well.

Beat the egg whites until stiff while gradually adding the remaining sugar. Then fold in the walnuts and carefully fold the meringue into the hot cider mixture until evenly mixed. Chill well before serving.

Danish Cider Pudding

Serves 6

3 cups fresh sweet cider
1 cup raspberry juice
1 cup sugar
Dash salt
6 tablespoons cornstarch

Pour 2 cups of cider and the raspberry juice into a saucepan. Stir in the sugar and salt and bring to a boil over high heat, stirring until the sugar is dissolved. Boil for one additional minute. Then dissolve the cornstarch in the remaining cider and pour it into the pan, stirring until the pudding thickens and clears. Remove from the heat at once. Chill thoroughly and serve with cream.

Soufflé Calvados

Serves 4

10 eggs, separated
⅔ cup sugar
½ cup Calvados
¼ teaspoon cream of tartar

Place 8 egg yolks in the top of a double boiler and bring the water below to a boil over high heat. Stir in the sugar and beat continuously for several minutes. Pour in the Calvados, stir, and then transfer the mixture to a bowl set in ice. Continue stirring until the mixture is thoroughly cooled.

Stir the cream of tartar into the 10 egg whites and beat vigorously until they are stiff. Carefully fold them into the Calvados mixture and pour into a greased soufflé dish. Bake at 400 degrees for 12 to 15 minutes or until the center is firm. Serve at once.

CHAPTER 4

Cider By The Glass

Even after cider takes its rightful place in the kitchen, it will probably remain at its most popular when it is served by the glass. And unlike most fruit juices, cider is easy to produce in quantity at home. A few apple trees, a small hand-operated press and a number of clean containers for storage, and the home cidermaker is ready to go to work.

Freshly pressed cider is delicious from the moment it leaves the apple, of course, as well as at the various stages in the process of natural fermentation. We usually freeze or chill and store a dozen gallons or more for use in the kitchen and for drinking as it naturally ferments. But the majority of the cider we have made in our backyard in the past ten years has been fermented with wine yeast, racked, bottled and re-fermented into a highly alcoholic, very dry, sparkling drink, much like champagne.

We serve this sparkling cider with fish, fowl and meat, enjoy it as an aperitif, and give it away at Christmas. Sparkling cider takes up much of our time in the winter and early spring, and attic space for half of the year. But it offers satisfaction found in very few other activities, perhaps because we initiate and complete every step of the process ourselves, from crushing the apples to popping the corks eight months later.

It all usually begins on a bright, crisp autumn morning, often chilly in that special way that recalls college football games and long walks through piles of leaves. That sort of weather seems to stimulate the kind of vigorous activity that making cider at home demands.

The orchard behind our small farmhouse is ready for harvest by late October. There are a dozen different trees, only two of which have been positively identified by variety. Little pruning has been done in the last several years, but nonetheless the branches are usually filled with fruit. Doubtless there are thousands of small orchards like ours across the U.S. and Canada. It is only necessary to spot a neglected tree or two, offer the owner some cider in trade for surplus fruit, and get access to a press in order to make your own cider.

A good cider press is truly a family treasure, valued by neighbors and friends as well as its owners for the efficiency and ease with which it separates the liquid from the apple pulp. Commercial presses are motorized for maximum productivity, but the most satisfying equipment for backyard use is the press that requires a strong back and shoulder.

Cider presses of various sizes at prices from $200 (U.S.) up, are available in farmers' supply centers, cooperative food outlets, hardware stores and lumberyards in almost any part of the country where apples are grown. Buyers can save some money by purchasing a press in kit form and putting it together themselves.

Most towns in apple-growing regions also offer cider-equipment rentals. Check with your local wine supply shop or food cooperative for information in your area.

No single clearinghouse exists for information on which of the dozens of models on the market are the most efficient and reliable. You can get good advice, though, by finding and quizzing other cider-makers, whose press experiences will be the most honest and useful consumer reports.

There are a few basic rules to remember when selecting a cider press. All of the moving parts should be made from cast iron (many of the less expensive models are made with aluminum). The press should be designed and mounted with a low center of gravity to keep the machinery as stationary as possible when in operation. A large fly-wheel should be used to turn the chipper, because the bigger the wheel, the easier it is to turn the crank.

It takes several strong backs to keep a hand-operated press going for an entire day. We are fortunate to have a dozen friends who practically stand in line to help us make cider. The fun and camaraderie of the event are certainly a drawing card, but the major incentive lies in the gallons of cider that everyone takes home at the end of the day. We try to press thirty-five to fifty gallons in a single day so that all of the helpers can share in the product and there will still be plenty left for us. (By *gallons* we mean U.S. gallons.)

An afternoon is spent earlier in the week collecting empty gallon jugs and bottles from local restaurants and taverns. Once a sufficient number are accumulated, the bottles are washed and rinsed thoroughly. A solution of sodium bisulfite is often used as a rinsing agent to chemically sterilize the bottles. Clean bottles are essential, as fresh cider will spoil quickly it if is put into dirty containers.

The clean jugs are stored in wooden crates and stacked by the press, which is located at the edge of the orchard. Our press has seen more than fifty seasons of ripened fruit. It is washed and dried carefully after every use and then stored wrapped in old sheets in a corner of the garden shed until the next autumn. The cast-iron crank, gears and fly-wheel that work together to turn the chipper are both awkward and difficult to get into motion, but once in operation the chipper grinds apples of all sizes with remarkable efficiency and uniformity.

Most of the volunteers last season were eager to put in a full day at the press and arrived ready for work by 9 a.m. Several agreed to climb three of the largest trees and gently shake the branches until the fruit dropped off. As the apple rain fell to the ground, a red carpet of apples spread throughout the orchard.

Then everyone grabbed wooden boxes and began to fill them with apples. There was no attempt to separate the fallen apples by type. We intended to use all of the available apples in our cider and leave varietal blending to the commercial producers. But we also knew from previous experience that our apples are generally tart and that the cider they produce makes a perfect base for alcoholic fermentation.

The filled boxes were stacked by the press. They were emptied by turns into a large tub and the apples were scrubbed clean. Then someone stepped up to the crank that turns the chipper and put the cumbersome machinery in motion. After a minute or so of concerted effort the chipper was turning at a rapid and even rate and a second worker began to throw apples one by one into the box above the rotating chipper. Within several minutes the burlap-lined basket underneath the chipper was filled with finely ground, juicy apple pulp. The basket was moved into a new position underneath the actual pressing end of the machine and a wooden round was placed on top. Someone turned the screw-like press until a stream of golden juice rushed from the basket, through a funnel lined with cheesecloth that removed extraneous pulp, and into a waiting jug.

We stood around the press and passed that first gallon from hand to hand, waving away thirsty yellow jackets with our free hand as we drank. Then we went back to work to fill the dozens of jugs that remained.

After the other cidermakers had gone home with compensation for their labor, there were twenty gallons of fresh cider left for us. We decided to make sparkling cider with ten gallons, which is also a good quantity for the beginning winemaker to work with. Ten gallons of fresh cider can be stored conveniently in two five-gallon carboys and monitored closely as it turns into wine. By working with two separately stored batches, the winemaker can vary the amount of sugar to a certain degree according to his taste. Finally, ten gallons will yield almost four cases of the finished product, enough to make the project worthwhile.

Several pieces of reusable hardware, in addition to the carboys, are required for ten gallons of sparkling cider. All the equipment and materials are available at a wine supply store. Champagne bottles can be recycled as they come through your kitchen or purchased for about $6 a case. Plastic corks and wires are required, as are airlocks for the carboys, a saccharometer to measure the sugar content of the fermenting wine, and a siphon hose. The total cost of this equipment should be less than $35 if you collect and reuse champagne bottles.

To make ten gallons of apple wine, which is the first step in making sparkling cider, you need 10 gallons of fresh sweet cider, 10 Campden tablets (sodium bisulphite), 2½ teaspoons of yeast nutrient, 2½ teaspoons of pectic enzyme powder, 10 to 14 pounds of sugar (20 to 28 cups), 10 grams of Montrachet wine yeast, and 10 rounded teaspoons of sparkolloid.

Each additive has a specific purpose in the winemaking process and must be carefully measured for predictable and successful results.

Campden tablets are used to kill the wild yeasts present in fresh cider, and to generally sterilize the process. Yeast nutrient contains the necessary nitrogen to encourage proper growth of the wine yeast. Wine yeast creates desirable fermentation by converting the naturally present and added sugar into alcohol. Pectic enzyme helps clarify the wine by breaking down the natural pectin. Sparkolloid, a derivative of seaweed, also enhances clarification.

Pour the cider into the carboys and add the Campden tablets, nutrient and pectic enzyme according to the directions on each package. Shake the carboy well and begin to add the sugar. The amount of sugar to be added will be determined by reading the saccharometer. To use the saccharometer, pour some cider from the carboy into a tall jar or glass and read the gauge on the side of the instrument.

Add sugar to the carboy and take readings with the saccharometer until it reads 24. The natural sweetness of the cider will determine just how much sugar should be added. Five gallons of cider will generally require from 5 to 7 pounds of sugar to register 24 Brix. That reading means that the finished wine will have a potential 11 percent alcohol with 2 percent residual sugar.

When all of the sugar and other additives have been added to the cider, the airlocks should be filled with water and put into place in the neck of each carboy. The cider can now be left alone for up to 72 hours in order to let the Campden tablets and the pectic enzyme go to work.

After 72 hours, the wine yeast, prepared according to the directions on the package, should be added to each carboy. The fermenting cider should be put in a room that is no cooler than 70 degrees in order to encourage the yeast. It will take at least six weeks for fermentation to be completed. Fermentation can take as long as twelve weeks, depending on the storage temperature and the activity of the wine yeast. Once a month has elapsed from the introduction of the wine yeast into the cider, it is wise to take a reading each week with the saccharometer.

When the reading is 4 or less, fermentation is almost done. Four percent residual sugar is great for sweet wine and 2 percent is considered dry.

The wine should be siphoned into clean carboys and the sparkolloid, prepared according to package directions, introduced. Temperature is no longer critical and the carboys can be moved to a cool location. The wine should be clear in three or four weeks.

This apple wine is perfectly drinkable and worth a small bottling, especially for the beginner. But it is also worth continuing the process through several more steps to get sparkling cider.

You will need 1 package of champagne yeast and 1½ pounds of sugar for each 5 gallons of apple wine. Pour 2 quarts of wine from each carboy and reserve. Then pour that gallon into a large pot, add 2 quarts of water and 1 pound of sugar, and bring the mixture to a boil, stirring well until the sugar is completely dissolved. Let the liquid cool to room temperature and then pour 1 quart of the liquid into a half-gallon bottle and the rest into a gallon bottle.

Start the champagne yeast in a bowl, according to the directions on the package. Once it is bubbling, add half of the wine mixture from the half-gallon bottle. Wait several minutes until the mixture begins to bubble and pour it b ck into the half-gallon bottle and shake well. Once the mixture in the half-gallon bottle begins to ferment, pour it into the gallon bottle and stir.

While you are waiting for the gallon bottle to show signs of fermentation, add the remaining sugar to the wine in the carboy. Then pour the mixture from the gallon bottle into the carboys as soon as activity is apparent.

It is absolutely essential that the champagne yeast be added to the wine in this manner. If it was added directly to the carboys, the wine would probably never clarify and would remain yeasty in taste because the yeast could not complete its work before being killed by the alcohol.

Once the wine in the carboys is actively fermenting, it may be bottled using champagne bottles, plastic corks and wire fasteners. The bottles should be stored in a cool place and turned upside-down so that the sediment produced in the fermentation process can be collected and disgorged. When all the sediment appears to be lodged on the cork (you can see it moving slowly down the neck), undo the wires and remove the cork, immediately placing your thumb over the opening. Right the bottle, top off with apple wine, and recork.

Bottle fermentation will usually be completed within three or four months, and the sparkling cider is then ready to drink. If it is stored carefully, though, in a cool, dark place, it can be held and enjoyed for as long as two years.

Although many would argue that fresh sweet cider is best when consumed in a pure and undiluted state, cider makes an excellent base for a wide variety of non-alcoholic and alcoholic drinks. The natural sweetness of cider makes the combination with tart fruit juices from berries or citrus fruits particularly tasty. That same quality makes cider a great base for punches, which when made with cider require little or no additional sugar.

Fresh cider, either chilled or warmed, blends especially well with eggs and cream. Its natural flavors are enhanced by such spices as cinnamon, nutmeg and cloves.

Cider and rum have been poured together for generations, and cider has also been mixed with a great variety of spirits from vodka to brandy. Most of these combinations are loaded with fresh fruit as well. Many are improved by using cider that is beginning to ferment.

The versatility of cider in the glass is almost as great as it is in the kitchen. We encourage you to try your own combinations.

Non-alcoholic Drinks

Apple Cherry Blend

Serves 4

1 cup tart cherry juice
3 cups sweet apple cider

Heat the cherry juice in a small saucepan over high heat until it begins to boil. Remove from the heat immediately and chill. Pour in the cider, stir well and serve.

Apple Raspberry Blend

Serves 4

3 cups fresh sweet cider
1 cup fresh raspberry juice

Combine the juices and stir well. Serve over ice or chill and add 2 cups ginger ale if desired. Try substituting apricot nectar or puréed strawberries for the raspberry juice.

Almond Milk

Serves 4

4 cups chilled fresh sweet cider
1 cup almonds, finely ground
2 tablespoons sesame seeds, finely ground
1 teaspoon Brazil nuts, finely ground
¾ teaspoon ground nutmeg
¾ teaspoon ground cinnamon
¾ teaspoon vanilla extract

Combine the cider with the almonds, sesame seeds and Brazil nuts and stir until smooth. Then stir in the nutmeg, cinnamon and vanilla. Strain to remove any lumps. Store in the refrigerator if not immediately used.

Banana Egg Smoothie

Serves 2

2 small bananas
2 eggs
2 cups chilled fresh sweet cider

Put the bananas in a blender and add the egg. Whirl at low speed, slowly pouring in the cider. Drink immediately.

Banana Yogurt Smoothie

Serves 2

1 cup plain yogurt
2 tablespoons honey
1 cup fresh sweet cider
1 small banana, cut into thin slices

Spoon the yogurt and honey into a blender. Whirl at low speed and add the egg. Add the banana slices and stir until thoroughly blended. Drink immediately. Strawberries can be substituted for the banana.

Cider Julep

Serves 4

2 cups fresh sweet cider
½ cup pineapple juice
1 cup orange juice
2 tablespoons lemon juice
Fresh mint leaves

Combine the cider and juices and stir well. Serve over ice and garnish with a mint leaf or two.

Cider Nog

Serves 4

2 eggs
2 tablespoons sugar
4 cups hot fresh sweet cider
Ground nutmeg

Beat the eggs and sugar until foamy and then pour in the cider. Beat for several minutes until very frothy. Pour into cups and garnish with nutmeg.

Cider/Orange Punch

Serves 8

½ cup sugar
1 cup fresh orange juice
¼ cup fresh lemon juice
¼ cup pineapple juice
6 cups fresh sweet cider

Combine the sugar, juices and cider and stir until thoroughly blended. Chill and serve.

Frothy Cider Cup

Serves 4

2 cups fresh sweet cider
1 cup orange juice
½ cup lemon juice
4 egg whites
2 teaspoons powdered sugar
Ground nutmeg

Pour the cider and juices into a blender. Whirl on low speed and add the egg whites and sugar. Increase speed and blend until very frothy. Pour into cups and garnish with nutmeg.

Hot Buttered Cider

Serves 4

2 cups fresh sweet cider
4 teaspoons brown sugar
2 tablespoons butter
4 3-inch cinnamon sticks

Bring the cider, sugar and butter nearly to a boil over medium-high heat in a large saucepan, stirring until the sugar is dissolved. Pour into serving cups and garnish with cinnamon.

Hot Mulled Cider

Serves 6

4 cups fresh apple cider
½ teaspoon whole cloves
½ teaspoon whole allspice
½ teaspoon ground nutmeg
2 3-inch cinnamon sticks
½ cup brown sugar

Heat the cider in a large saucepan, add the spices and sugar and simmer over medium heat for 5 minutes. Serve warm.

Ice Cream Cider Float

Serves 6

6 cups fresh sweet cider
½ teaspoon ground allspice
1 4-inch cinnamon stick
8 whole cloves
¼ cup brown sugar
1 tablespoon grated lemon rind
6 tablespoons vanilla ice cream

Pour the cider into a large saucepan and place over medium-low heat. Add the spices and stir in the sugar. Simmer for 5 minutes, stirring constantly, until the sugar dissolves. Then add the lemon rind, remove the cloves and cinnamon and chill thoroughly. Serve in cups topped with 1 tablespoon of ice cream.

Honey Cider Shake

Serves 4

2 cups fresh sweet cider
1 cup orange juice
2 tablespoons honey
1 teaspoon grated orange rind

Pour cider and juice into a blender and whirl at low speed. Add the honey and orange rind and blend thoroughly. Serve over ice.

Hot Cider and Cream

Serves 4

2 cups fresh sweet cider
½ cup heavy cream
2 teaspoons sugar
Ground nutmeg
Grated semi-sweet or powdered chocolate

Heat the cider in a small saucepan over medium heat until bubbles form at the edge of the pan. Whip the cream in a small bowl, adding the sugar gradually, until the cream is stiff. Pour the cider into a cup. Top with cream, nutmeg and chocolate.

Wassail

Serves 10

2 quarts eggnog
1 quart fresh sweet cider
¼ teaspoon ground nutmeg
¼ teaspoon ground cinnamon
2 whole cloves
½ teaspoon grated lemon peel
Whipped cream
Nutmeg

Combine the eggnog, cider, nutmeg, cinnamon, cloves and lemon peel in a large saucepan. Heat over low heat, stirring occasionally. Serve either warm or chilled with whipped cream and nutmeg sprinkled on top.

Alcoholic Drinks

Although many of the non-alcoholic cider drinks improve nicely with a shot of rum or dash of sherry, there are a number of alcoholic drinks that are specifically concocted with cider as the featured mixer. Some of them have silly names and most are surprisingly tasty.

Apple Knocker

Serves 1

1 ounce bourbon
4 ounces fresh sweet cider
Dash Angostura bitters
Apple slices, orange slices, lime wedges

Pour the bourbon and cider over ice in a large glass. Add the bitters and stir. Garnish with fresh fruit.

Apple Snap

Serves 1

2 ounces brandy
2 ounces fresh sweet cider
2 ounces 7-Up or other lemon soda
Lemon slices

Pour the brandy and cider over ice in a tall glass. Stir and add the soda. Garnish with fresh lemon.

Cider Cooler

Serves 1

½ ounce creme de menthe
1 ounce vodka
3 ounces fresh sweet cider
¼ cup crushed ice
Strip cucumber rind

Pour liqueur, vodka, cider and ice into a blender. Blend on high speed until thoroughly mixed. Pour into a glass and garnish with cucumber.

Cranberry Surprise

Serves 1

1 ounce vodka
4 ounces fresh sweet cider
2 ounces cranberry juice
Lime or lemon slice

Pour vodka, cider and cranberry juice together and stir until well blended. Pour into a tall glass over ice and garnish with fruit slice.

Rum Cider Tonic

Serves 1

1 ounce dark rum
3 ounces fresh sweet cider
2 ounces tonic water
Thin lemon slice

Pour the rum into a tall glass filled with ice. Add the cider and tonic and stir until well mixed. Garnish with lemon slice.

Black Snake

Serves 1

1 ounce blackberry brandy
2 ounces bottled cider
Lemon slice

Pour the brandy into a short glass filled with ice. Then pour in the cider and stir well. Garnish with lemon slice.

Champagne Cocktail

Serves 1

1 teaspoon sugar
Dash Angostura bitters
4 ounces chilled bottled cider
1 ounce peach brandy

Place the sugar in the bottom of a champagne glass and saturate with bitters. Pour in the cider, then the brandy, and stir.

Diamond Fizz

Serves 1

4 ounces chilled bottled cider
2 lemon slices
1 ounce brandy

Pour the cider into a chilled champagne glass. Put in the lemon slices and add the brandy. Shake gently to mix.

Egg Flip

Serves 3

1 pint bottled cider
1 egg
1 heaping tablespoon sugar

Heat the cider in a small saucepan, but do not boil. Beat the egg and sugar until it is frothy and pour in half of the cider, beating continuously. Then add this mixture to the remaining cider, taking care not to boil the drink or it will curdle.

Hot Lemon Cider

Serves 4

1 quart bottled cider
2 ounces sugar
2 large lemons

Pour the cider into a large saucepan and place over medium heat. Strip the peel from the lemons and stir into the cider while it is heating. Squeeze the juice into the sugar. Then add the sugar to the cider. Garnish with fresh lemon peel.

Merton College Cider Cup

Serves 10

1 26-ounce bottle dry hard cider, chilled
½ pint dry sherry, chilled
4 ounces brandy
Sugar
Ground nutmeg
1 lemon, cut into thin slices
Fresh mint leaves

Combine the cider, sherry and brandy with ice in a large bowl. Sweeten to taste, sprinkle with nutmeg, and garnish with lemon and mint.

Tomato Refresher

Serves 2

1 cup tomato juice
1 cup dry hard cider
1 teaspoon lemon juice

Combine the juices and cider. Stir well and serve over ice.

Index